Sinful Smoothies

Sinful Smoothies

More Than 130 Dessert Smoothies
and Other Indulgences

Donna Pliner Rodnitzky

THREE RIVERS PRESS
NEW YORK

Published by Three Rivers Press, New York, New York. Member of the Crown Publishing Group, a division of Random House, Inc.
www.crownpublishing.com

THREE RIVERS PRESS and the Tugboat design are registered trademarks of Random House, Inc.

Various recipes have been previously published in the following works by the author: *Ultimate Smoothies* (Prima, 2000), *Summer Smoothies* (Prima, 2002), *Slim Smoothies* (Prima, 2003), and *Tipsy Smoothies* (Three Rivers Press, 2003).

Printed in the United States of America

Design by Karen Minster

Library of Congress Cataloging-in-Publication Data
Rodnitzky, Donna.
    Sinful smoothies : more than 130 dessert smoothies and other indulgences / Donna Pliner Rodnitzky.—1st ed.
    1. Blenders (Cookery).   2. Smoothies (Beverages).   I. Title.
TX840.B5R62697   2004
641.8'7—dc22   2003021020

ISBN 0-7615-2582-3

10 9 8 7 6 5 4 3 2 1

First Edition

With affection and heartfelt thanks

to my husband, Bob, who has
been my greatest and most
enthusiastic supporter for more
than thirty years. Without his
unconditional praise and generous
encouragement in all my
endeavors, I might not have been
able to write *Sinful Smoothies,*
as well as all my other books.
I also feel blessed to have
three extraordinary children,
David, Adam, and Laura.
Their hard work, perseverance,
and dedication to excellence
in everything they do are
a constant source of pride.

Acknowledgments

Among the pleasures I've had writing cookbooks for Prima Publishing/Random House has been the opportunity to work with a team of very exceptional people. I am grateful to acquisitions editor Denise Sternad for her relentless pursuit of unique ideas for novel cookbooks—*Sinful Smoothies* being no exception. I am also indebted to my project editor, Michelle McCormack, who has been such a joy to work with these past years. Now that Prima's cookbook publishing activity has been transferred to other publishing units of Random House, I feel very fortunate that this book's production will be in the very competent hands of associate editor Caroline Sincerbeaux of the Crown Publishing Group. Thanks to Sandra Schmeil, cover designer, and the entire staff at Three Rivers Press for their excellent professionalism in bringing this book to publication.

I would also like to thank Sugar Mark and Judy Neiman for sharing their sauce and garnish recipes with me.

Contents

Introduction

*All the things I really like to do
are either immoral, illegal or fattening.*

—ALEXANDER WOOLLCOTT (1887–1943)
American author and critic

IT IS EASY TO UNDERSTAND THE SKYROCKETING success of smoothies. These fruit-filled delights are not only inherently flavorful, they provide significant health benefits as well. As tasty and healthful as your favorite smoothie may be, though, from time to time you may crave something a bit more luxurious and self-indulgent. The unadorned fruity flavors of a standard smoothie simply will not satisfy your sweet tooth. To successfully yield to these repressed impulses, you need not resort to a mouthful of cookies or a candy bar. Discover in these pages how a smoothie can be reinvented as a sinfully rich and satisfyingly sweet indulgence. Get ready for an exhilarating experience. Peaches blended with a delectable caramel sauce, bananas melded with creamy coffee gelato, and juicy pineapple combined with rum and coconut ice cream are just a few examples of the temptations that await you. You'll be amazed at how simply adding a few irresistibly rich ingredients to a humble smoothie can result in an opulent treat. Rejoice! Such sinfully delicious terms as "sumptuous," "creamy," and "richly flavored" can now be added back to the smoothie lover's vocabulary.

Sinful Smoothies appropriately begins with a chapter entitled "The Cream of the Crop." In that section, you will discover the secrets of selecting and preparing the best fruits for the ultimate sinful smoothie. To become more familiar with the equipment you will need, the next chapter, "Not for the Faint of Heart: Making a Sinful Smoothie," will prove very useful. That chapter concentrates on the essential tools needed to transform your kitchen into a wickedly efficient source of ravishing treats. You will also discover a host of helpful techniques that will enable you to elevate every sinful smoothie masterpiece you prepare to the absolute pinnacle of frosty seduction.

The three chapters that follow are devoted to mouthwatering smoothie recipes. For example, you'll be tempted by the more than forty recipes in the first of these chapters, "Sumptuous Delights: Just Enough Sweetness in a Glass." These delectable smoothies are not quite as decadent as some found later in the book, but they are made with enough rich ingredients to satisfy most cravings you may have for something that's naughty. Two of my favorite creations are Jitterbug Smoothie, made with espresso, hazelnut-flavored syrup, banana, and chocolate ice cream; and Raspberry Clementine Euphoria, made with juicy clementines, raspberries, and Godiva White Chocolate Raspberry ice cream. Both are a fantasy come true.

The next chapter, "Ultimate Indulgences: Make Mine Thick and Rich," contains more than forty recipes that are clearly over-the-top. Each one is a celebration of luscious ingredients that will leave you begging for more. Imagine sipping a strawful of Banana and Macadamia Praline Seduction, comprised of banana, Chocolate Sauce, coarsely chopped macadamia nut praline, and Almond Joy ice cream. Another heart-stopper is Pineapple, Banana, and Praline Temptation, made with Praline Sauce, banana, pineapple, and pralines and cream ice cream.

The frosty creations in chapter 5, "Happy Hour Smoothies: Cocktails That Satisfy Your Sweet Tooth," are made with traditional smoothie ingredients bolstered by your favorite alcoholic libation and some seductively sweet additions. You'll find that these wonderful creations not only serve as a perfect pre- or postmeal cocktail, but when accented with an edible garnish can also grace an elegant dessert plate. If you've never indulged in a Bananas Foster smoothie, you are in for a delectable surprise. This sinful delight contains bananas, rum, crème de banana liqueur, and vanilla ice cream. One of my favorite happy hour smoothies is Heather's Dream Smoothie, made with Sambuca liqueur, peaches, vanilla ice cream, and, of course, three coffee beans for good luck.

Chapter 6, "Sinful Sauces and Toppings: Beyond Chocolate Fudge," contains a fabulous array of recipes for sassy sauces to endow any smoothie with a more sensual taste, as well as toppings and fillings to add crunch and rich flavor.

Finally, chapter 7, "Great Garnishes: Go to the Head of the Glass," contains recipes for edible garnishes that will enable you to present any of your favorite sinful smoothie creations in a visually striking and impressive manner.

The recipes featured in this book will convince you that smoothies can easily be transformed from frosty and fruity to feisty. Whether you indulge in one of these sensuous delights alone, share it with family and friends, or sip it with a special someone, you're due for some excitement in a glass.

1

The Cream of the Crop

How to Select, Prepare, and Store Fresh Fruit

I love fruit, when it is expensive.

—SIR ARTHUR WING PINERO
(1855–1934)
English dramatist

FRESH FRUIT IS AN IMPORTANT COMPONENT OF A smoothie, even a sinful one, and it is worth the effort to select the freshest fruit available. For this reason, you must become well informed about the wide variety of available orchard bounty in order to create the perfect smoothie. The objective of this chapter is to acquaint you with these delectable bundles of flavor and guide you in choosing, storing, and preparing fruit. It is important to never make a choice based on fruit's appearance alone. At first glance, a peach may look ripe because of its rich color. But a number of less obvious attributes are equally important to qualify a peach as smoothie ready. First, determine whether the fruit has a fresh aroma. How heavy or dense is it? Is it firm, yet resilient to the touch? These characteristics are often more important than the fruit's color. The good news is that once you become a fruit connoisseur, you will find that it's actually quite easy to determine whether fruit is ripe and smoothie ready or not.

I am certain that as you become more familiar with the wide array of fruit available, you will delight in the excitement of including them in this new generation of deliciously enticing smoothies. As you navigate the aisles of your favorite farmer's market or produce department, I hope you find the following information useful in your quest for the best nature has to offer.

APPLE

Apples are believed to have originated in Central Asia and the Caucasus, but they have been cultivated since prehistoric times. They were brought to the United States at the beginning of the seventeenth century and later to Africa and Australia. Today, more than a hundred varieties of apples are commercially grown in the United States.

Apples, whether red, green, or yellow, all have a firm, crisp flesh. They are a rich source of fiber. Some apples have a sweet flavor with a hint of tartness, while others are less sweet and more tart. Most apples are delicious when made into a smoothie, but your flavor preference will determine the best variety for you.

Selection
When choosing an apple, look for one that is firm and crisp with a smooth, tight skin. Most important,

the apple should have a sweet-smelling aroma. Avoid any apple that has a bruised or blemished skin. Buy the organic variety whenever possible. Most nonorganic apples are heavily sprayed with pesticides and later waxed to preserve and keep them looking fresh. This can potentially affect the taste, not to mention your health. Should you find a worm in an organic apple, simply remove the unwelcome visitor when you cut the apple, thereby removing any health or aesthetic concerns. Wash all apples in cool water and dry them well before cutting. Uncut apples can be stored in the crisper bin of the refrigerator for up to six weeks if they are kept separate from other fruits and vegetables.

APRICOT

The apricot is a round or oblong fruit measuring about two inches in diameter with skin and flesh that are golden orange in color. It is a very sweet and juicy fruit with a single, smooth stone. The apricot is native to northern China and was known to be a food source as early as 2200 B.C.

Selection

When choosing apricots, look for those that are well colored, plump, and fairly firm but yield slightly when gently pressed. An apricot that is soft to the touch and juicy is fully ripe and should be eaten or used in a smoothie right away. If an apricot is hard, it can be placed in a brown paper bag and allowed to ripen at room temperature for a day or two. Avoid any that are green or yellow in color as they may not yet be ripe. Refrigerate ripe apricots in the crisper bin of the refrigerator for up to a week. Wash them in cool water just before you are ready to use them.

BANANA

The banana has been around for so long that according to Hindu legend, it was actually the forbidden fruit of the Garden of Eden. It also is believed that the banana was widely cultivated throughout Asia and Oceania before recorded history and that the Spanish colonists introduced banana shoots to the New World in 1516.

Selection

Bananas are picked when they are green and sweeten as they ripen. When choosing a banana, look for one that is completely yellow. The riper a banana, or the more yellow its skin, the sweeter it is. Yellow bananas with green tips and green necks or bananas that are all yellow with light green necks also are ready to eat and use in a smoothie. Green bananas will ripen at room temperature in two or three days. Alternatively, they can be placed in a brown paper bag to accelerate the ripening process. If you add a tomato or apple to the bag, the bananas will ripen even faster. (Fruit cells produce a colorless gas, called ethylene, which stimulates ripening in many fruits and some vegetables. When a banana and an apple or tomato are placed in the same bag, the ethylene from the apple or tomato will help ripen the banana.) Ripe bananas can be stored at room temperature or in the refrigerator for a couple of days.

BLACKBERRY

The blackberry is a small black, blue, or dark red berry that grows on thorny bushes (brambles). These berries are oblong in shape and grow up to one inch in length. The United States is the world's dominant producer of blackberries. Blackberries are at their peak in flavor and availability from June through September, but may still be found in some supermarkets from November on into April.

Selection

When choosing blackberries, look for ones that are plump and solid with full color and a bright, fresh appearance. Place them in a shallow container to prevent the berries on top from crushing those on the bottom. Cover the container and store it in the crisper bin of the refrigerator for one to two days. Wash blackberries in cool water just before you are ready to use them.

BLUEBERRY

Native to North America, the blueberry has the distinction of being the second most popular berry in the United States. It has been around for thousands of years but was not cultivated until the turn of the twentieth century. Today, 95 percent of the world's commercial crop of blueberries is grown in the United States. Blueberries are at their peak in flavor from mid-April to late September. They are available in the southern states first and gradually move north as the season progresses.

Selection

When choosing blueberries, look for those that are plump and firm with a dark blue color and a silvery bloom. The bloom on blueberries is the dusty powder that protects them from the sun; it does not rinse off. Avoid any berries that appear dull, as this may indicate that the fruit is old. Blueberries should be prepared in the same way as blackberries, washed just prior to use, but they can be stored for a longer time in the crisper bin of the refrigerator, from three to five days.

CHERRY

Cherries are small, round, red to black, and occasionally yellow fruit that grow on a tree. There are numerous varieties, but all of them fall into one of three categories: sweet, sour, or a hybrid of the two. Cherries grow in the temperate zones of Europe, Asia, and the Americas. It is believed that they originated in northeastern Asia and later spread throughout the temperate zones in prehistory carried by birds that ate the cherries and later dropped the stones. Cherries are available from late May through early August.

Selection

When choosing cherries, look for those that are dark red, plump, and firm with an attached stem. Store them in the crisper bin of the refrigerator for up to two days, and wash them in cool water just before you are ready to use them.

MANGO

Mangoes were cultivated in India and the Malay Archipelago as long as four thousand years ago. In the 1700s and 1800s, European explorers introduced the fruit to other tropical areas. Mangoes were first raised in the United States some time in the early 1900s.

The mango resembles a peach in appearance but is more elongated in shape. It has a thin, leathery skin that is waxy and smooth, and its color can be green, red, orange, yellow, or any combination. The skin surrounds a very aromatic and juicy pulp and a hard inner pit.

Selection

When choosing a mango, look for one that is very fragrant and plump around the stem area and gives slightly when pressed. No matter what the color of the mango, the best-flavored ones will have a yellow tinge when ripe. Mangoes also can be ripened at room temperature. To accelerate the process, place the mango and an apple in a brown paper bag and leave on the kitchen counter overnight. Once it has ripened, it can be stored in the crisper bin of the refrigerator for up to five days.

ORANGE

Fresh oranges are widely grown in Florida, California, and Arizona and are available all year long. The two major varieties are Valencia and navel. Two other varieties grown in the western states are Cara Cara and Moro (similar to the blood orange), both of which are available throughout the winter months.

Selection

When selecting an orange, look for one that is heavy for its size and firm. Avoid oranges with a bruised skin, indicating possible fermentation, as well as those with a loose skin, suggesting they may be dry inside. Although oranges can be stored at room temperature for a few days, their flavor is best when kept in the crisper bin of the refrigerator.

PEACH

Grown since prehistoric times, peaches were first cultivated in China. They were later introduced into Europe and Persia. It is believed that the Spaniards brought peaches to North, Central, and South America. The Spanish missionaries planted the first peach trees in California.

Numerous varieties of peaches are available, and they are broken down into rough classifications. One type of peach is the freestone, so named because the pit separates easily from the peach. Another variety is the clingstone, in which the pit is firmly attached to the fruit. The freestone is the peach most often found in supermarkets because it is easy to eat, while clingstones are frequently canned.

Selection

When picking peaches, look for ones that are relatively firm with a fuzzy, creamy yellow skin and a sweet aroma. The pink blush on the peach indicates its variety, not its ripeness. Avoid peaches with a wrinkled skin or those that are soft or blemished. A ripe peach should yield gently when touched. To ripen peaches, keep them at room temperature and out of direct sunlight until the skin yields slightly to the touch. Once they are ripe, store them in a single layer in the crisper bin of the refrigerator for up to five days. Wash peaches in cool water just before you are ready to use them.

PEAR

Pear is the name of a tree of the rose family and its fruit. It is believed that pears were eaten by Stone Age people. However, the pears we are accustomed to eating were first cultivated in southeastern Europe and western Asia as recently as 2000 B.C. Pear trees were introduced to the Americas when European settlers arrived in the 1700s.

Selection

Pears are a unique fruit because they ripen best off the tree. This explains why they are often so hard when you purchase them at the supermarket. Many pears have stickers that tell you the stage of ripeness, such as READY TO EAT or LET ME RIPEN FOR TWO DAYS. When choosing pears, look for ones that are firm and unblemished with a fresh pear aroma. To ripen pears, place them in a brown paper bag at room temperature for a few days. To kick-start the ripening process, place pears in a brown paper bag with a ripe banana or an apple. When they yield to gentle thumb pressure, the pears are ready to eat. Wash ripe pears in cool water and store them in the crisper bin of the refrigerator for two to five days.

PINEAPPLE

The pineapple is a tropical fruit that is native to Central and South America. In 1493, Christopher Columbus discovered pineapples growing on the island of Guadeloupe and brought them back to Spain. By the 1700s, pineapples were being grown in greenhouses throughout Europe.

Selection

When choosing a pineapple, look for one that has a fresh pineapple aroma at the stem end and a crown with crisp, fresh-looking green leaves. It should also be plump and symmetrical in size. Avoid any pineapples that have soft spots or discolorations. A ripe pineapple can be stored at room temperature for up to two days, or the fruit can be cut from the shell and refrigerated in an airtight container for three to five days.

RASPBERRY

It is believed that red raspberries spread all over Europe and Asia in prehistoric times. Because they were so delicious growing wild, it was not until the 1600s that raspberries were actually cultivated in Europe. Those cultivated in North America originated from two groups: the red raspberry, native to Europe, and the wild red variety, native to North America.

Selection

When choosing raspberries, it is always best to buy them when they are in season—usually starting in late June and lasting four to six weeks. If you are fortunate enough to have a local berry farm, take advantage of it by visiting at the beginning of the season to get the best pick. Select berries that are large and plump, bright, shiny, uniform in color, and free of mold. Avoid any that are mushy. Before refrigerating raspberries, carefully go through the batch and discard any that show signs of spoilage. Place the raspberries in a shallow container to prevent the berries on top from crushing those on the bottom. Cover the container and store it in the crisper bin of the refrigerator for one to two days. Wash raspberries in cool water just before you are ready to use them.

STRAWBERRY

Strawberries date as far back as 2,200 years ago. They are known to have grown wild in Italy in the third century, and by 1588, they were discovered in Virginia by the first European settlers. Local Indians cultivated the strawberry as early as the mid-1600s, and by the middle of the nineteenth century, this fruit was widely grown in many parts of North America.

The strawberry grows in groups of three on the stem of a plant that is very low to the ground. As the fruit ripens, it changes from greenish white in color to a lush flame red. The strawberry does not have a skin but is actually covered by hundreds of tiny seeds.

Selection

The best time to buy strawberries is in June and July when they are at their peak of juicy freshness. As with raspberries, if you are lucky enough to live near a strawberry farm, a pick-your-own day trip is a wonderful family outing as well as an excellent way to get the very best of the crop. Look for plump, firm, and deep-colored fruit with a bright green cap and a sweet strawberry aroma. Strawberries can be stored in a single layer in the crisper bin of the refrigerator for up to two days. Wash them with their caps in cool water just before you are ready to use them.

TANGERINE

Tangerines, also known as Mandarins, are a close cousin of the orange. Native to Southeastern Asia, they have been widely cultivated in orange-growing regions of the world. While tangerines resemble an orange, they are smaller in size and oblong in shape but can be slightly flat on each end. Another variety of tangerine is the clementine, sometimes called an Algerian tangerine. Clementines are a cross between Mandarin oranges and Seville oranges and are usually seedless. Because all tangerines have a loose, puffy skin, these sweet, juicy fruits peel easily, and their sections can be readily separated.

Selection

Choose tangerines that have a deep, glossy orange skin and are heavy for their size. Tangerines are usually ripe and ready to eat when you buy them, but they can be left on the kitchen counter for up to one week at a cool room temperature and then stored in the crisper bin of the refrigerator away from vegetables for up to two weeks.

FREEZING FRUIT

Because fruit is so perishable, you may want to freeze some while it is in season in order to store for later use. By purchasing an ample quantity to freeze, you can be certain of having on hand a supply of any fruit you know will not be available after a certain date when you need it to prepare one of your favorite smoothies. Also, there may be times when already ripened fruit isn't needed immediately. Freezing prevents overripening and allows fruit to be utilized at a later time.

To make a sinful smoothie with the optimal consistency, it is important that you freeze for thirty minutes or more any fresh fruit you use. Using partially frozen fruit also helps maintain your smoothie at an ideal icy-cold temperature.

Whether you are freezing for immediate use or for storage, the basic preparation is identical.

- When you are ready to freeze **cherries** and **apricots** (which should be cut in half and their stones removed) or **berries**, place them in a colander and rinse with a gentle stream of cool water. Pat them dry with a paper towel.

- To freeze a **peach** (remove its stone) or a **pear** (remove its stem and seeds), wash and then cut it into small pieces.

- To freeze a **banana,** remove its skin and either slice it or freeze it whole and then slice it later, before you use it.

- Before freezing **oranges** and **clementines** (or **tangerines**), remove the peel and pith, break each into segments, and remove any seeds.

- To prepare **apples** and **mangoes** for freezing, remove their peels and seeds or pits before cubing.

- When you are ready to freeze a **pineapple,** remove its top, the outer layering, and the core, then cut into cubes.

Place the prepared fruit on a baking sheet lined with freezer paper, plastic-coated side facing up to prevent it from sticking to the surface. (In a pinch, non-stick aluminum foil or parchment paper can be used instead.) If you are storing the fruit to use at a later date, transfer the frozen pieces to an airtight plastic bag large enough to hold them in a single layer. Label the contents and mark the date on the bag, and freeze for up to two weeks. Most fruit can be kept in the freezer that long without a loss of flavor. If you are preparing fruit for immediate use, freeze it for at least thirty minutes, after which time it will be ready to add to your other smoothie ingredients.

HOW MUCH FRUIT SHOULD I BUY?

To determine how much fruit you will need to make a sinful smoothie, consult the list below for an estimate of the quantity of fruit you'll actually end up with once the skin, hull, seeds, pit, and core are removed. You can use the average weight per individual fruit provided in the table or, to be more precise, you can weigh the fruit, using the supermarket scale, before you purchase it.

FRUIT	How Much to Buy	Average Weight	Number of Cups
Apple	1 medium	6 ounces	1 cup
Apricots	3	8 ounces	1 cup
Banana	1 large	10 ounces	1 cup
Blackberries	½ pint	6 ounces	1 ¼ cups
Blueberries	½ pint	8 ounces	1 cup
Cherries	19 to 20	8 ounces	1 cup
Mango	1 medium	10 ounces	1 cup
Orange	1 medium	10 ounces	1 cup
Peach	1 medium	8 ounces	1 cup
Pear	1 medium	6 ounces	1 cup
Pineapple	1 medium	3 pounds	5 ½ cups
Raspberries	1 box	6 ounces	1 ¼ cups
Strawberries	7 to 8 medium	6 ounces	1 cup
Tangerine	1 small	5 ounces	½ cup

2

Not for the Faint of Heart

Making a Sinful Smoothie

It's a poor workman who blames his tools.
—ENGLISH PROVERB

THE GOOD NEWS IS THAT IT ISN'T NECESSARY to have an extensive array of equipment in your kitchen to prepare a sinful smoothie. In fact, all you need is a modest number of tools: a sharp knife for prepping fruit, measuring spoons and cups, a rubber spatula to remove every last drop from the blender, airtight freezer bags for storing freshly cut fruit in the freezer, and, of course, the essential blender. There are, in addition, a couple of optional items that you might want to consider. As you glance through the garnish recipes found in this cookbook, you will note the mention of two useful tools that may not be standard equipment in your kitchen. The first, a silicone mat, is a reusable laminated food-grade silicone sheet with a nonstick surface. It can be used to line a baking sheet for making cookies, cakes, and pastries, or as a countertop surface when working with gum paste, caramelized syrup, chocolate, or fondant. The second is a mandoline slicer. It is a handheld kitchen implement containing a variety of cartridge blades that perform precision cutting of foods in several modes such as very thick, very thin, and julienne, just to mention a few. These are very useful items, but neither is an absolute necessity. Finally, although a food processor can be used to make a smoothie, most smoothie experts would agree that a blender is definitely the preferred appliance. A food processor can be used to purée fruit and ice, but it often leaves small chunks of ice behind. A blender breaks up the ice and fruit into tiny particles and is better able to process liquids and solids into a fine, smooth, and well-aerated purée.

THE BLENDER

The blender is by far the most important piece of kitchen equipment when it comes to making a proper smoothie. Credit for the invention of this indispensable appliance goes to Stephen J. Poplawski, who, in 1922, first conceived of placing a spinning blade at the bottom of a glass container. By 1935, Fred Waring and Frederick Osius had made significant improvements on the original design and began marketing the Waring Blender. The rest is history.

A blender basically consists of a tall, narrow stainless steel, plastic, or glass food container fitted with metal blades at the bottom. These blades usually have four cutting edges placed on two or four planes, allowing for the ingredients in the container to hit multiple cutting surfaces. The rapidly spinning blades cause an upward motion, creating a vortex in the container that allows for the incorporation of more air in the final product, giving it a smoother consistency.

When selecting a blender, you should assess certain basic qualities, including its durability, ease of operation and cleaning, capacity, and noise production. With such a wide variety of blenders to choose from, I hope the following information will help you narrow your choice.

- Blender containers typically come in two sizes: thirty-two ounces and forty ounces. If you will routinely be preparing smoothies for more than two people, choose the larger one.

- Blender motors come in different sizes. Those with 290-watt motors are adequate for most blending jobs, but not optimal for smoothies. Those with 330- to 400-watt motors, considered to be of professional caliber, are excellent for crushing ice, a very important feature for creating the best smoothies.

- Blenders can be found with a variety of blade speed options, ranging from two speeds (high and low) to multiple (between five and fourteen) speeds. Variable-speed models provide more options, such as the ability to liquefy and whip.

- The blender should have a removable bottom for ease of cleaning.

- Container lids should have a secondary lid that can be easily removed. This allows for the addition of ingredients while the blender is turned on.

- Avoid plastic container jars because they become scratched over time and do not wash well in the dishwasher.

Recently, new blenders specifically designed for making smoothies have become available. One whirring wizard, called the Smoothie Elite (by Back to Basics), has several useful features, including a custom stir stick to break up the air pockets, an ice-crunching blade that assures consistent smoothie texture, and a convenient spigot at the bottom of the container that serves up the finished product.

Although a blender is the ideal appliance for making smoothies, you may prefer a food processor because of its overall versatility or, more important, because it is an appliance that you already own. The *New York Times* described the food processor as the "twentieth-century French revolution." This unique appliance can mince, chop, grate, shred, slice, knead, blend, purée, liquefy, and crush ice.

Unlike the blender container, the food processor bowl is wide and low, causing food to be sent sideways rather than upward by the spinning blade. This motion results in food striking the sides of the container, with less incorporation of air than in the upward motion produced by a blender. Still, if it's all you have, it should do fine. Your smoothies just won't be as perfect.

Once you have decided on the features you would like in a blender, I encourage you to visit several appliance or department stores and personally view the various models available. The salesclerk should be able to provide you with information to help you make the best decision. The Internet is another resource. Many of the companies that manufacture these appliances have very informative sites describing their individual product, and some also provide a phone number so you can speak to a representative. Finally, *Consumer Reports* and similar publications provide comparison quality ratings of a variety of blenders.

HELPFUL TECHNIQUES

Now that the blender (or food processor) has taken its rightful place, center stage on your countertop, it is time to rev it up and make a sinful smoothie. I hope you found equipping your kitchen with the necessary tools to make smoothies a relatively easy process. You will be pleased to learn that mastering the techniques required to prepare them is no more difficult. In fact, preparing a smoothie may be one of the most uncomplicated tasks you will ever perform in your kitchen. All you do is simply place the appropriate smoothie ingredients in a blender and you will end up with a wonderfully delicious final product. However, for those who want to create the truly perfect sinful smoothie, there are a few additional helpful techniques that I have discovered that will help you reach that lofty goal.

- To get the most delicious fruit, buy it when it is in season and at peak flavor.

- Before freezing fruit, wash and dry or peel it, then follow the preparation instructions given in the previous chapter.

- Store-bought individually frozen fruit can be substituted for fresh frozen fruit, but it should be used within six months of the purchase date. Avoid using frozen fruit packaged in sweetened syrup.

- To be certain that you have a supply of your favorite seasonal fruits, stock up before they are no longer available for purchase. Although fruits have the most flavor when they are kept frozen for only one to two weeks, they can be kept in the freezer for a slightly longer amount of time and still be edible.

- If the fruit you have frozen becomes clumped together, gently pound it within the sealed bag with a mallet or blunt object until the pieces have separated.

- When adding ingredients to a blender, always add the liquid first, then the frozen fruit, and the ice cream last. Start the blender on low speed to crush the fruit and blend the mixture. Gradually increase the speed until the mixture is smooth. It takes three to four minutes for a smoothie to reach its optimal consistency. It may be necessary to turn off the blender periodically and stir the mixture with a spoon, working from the bottom up.

- If the smoothie is too thin, add more fruit. Conversely, if the smoothie is too thick, add more of your favorite juice, milk, or spirit.

3

Sumptuous Delights

Just Enough Sweetness in a Glass

Ice cream is exquisite. What a pity it isn't illegal.

—VOLTAIRE (FRANÇOIS-MARIE AROUET)
(1694–1778)
French philosopher

FOR MANY OF US, NOTHING IS MORE REFRESHING
and soul-satisfying than a simple smoothie made
with fruit juice and fruit. But sometimes you might
welcome a subliminal touch of sweetness, yet don't
want to acquiesce to total debauchery. A scoop of
sensuous coffee gelato, a touch of rich mascarpone
cheese, or a few tablespoons of seductive caramel
sauce added to your favorite fruits may be all you
need to take this first small step toward nirvana.
Read on to find an impressively long list of potential
pleasure-enhancing ingredients.

As you glance through this chapter, you will be
delighted to find how easy it is to edge a humble
smoothie just a little closer to pure decadence. Go
ahead and test the waters. I predict that once you

have experienced the ultimate pleasure of a small splurge on such smoothie creations as Apple Pie à la Mode, showcasing sautéed apples, cinnamon, and apple pie ice cream, or Banana and Peanut Butter Obsession, featuring a banana, peanut butter, and chocolate–peanut butter ice cream, you'll find it hard not to sample all forty tantalizing smoothie recipes in this chapter.

Apple Pie à la Mode

Who doesn't love a slice of warm apple pie with a scoop of ice cream on top? Well, this deliciously thick, chilled apple pie smoothie is the next best thing. Be sure to double or triple the apple filling mixture so you can have it ready the next time you have a craving for this all-time favorite comfort food.

1 SERVING

2 tablespoons (¼ stick) unsalted butter
1 ½ cups peeled and diced apple
1 tablespoon sugar
¼ teaspoon ground cinnamon
½ to ⅔ cup apple juice or milk
1 teaspoon honey, or to taste (optional)
½ cup apple pie or favorite vanilla ice cream

Line a baking sheet with freezer paper. Set aside.

Melt the butter in a medium sauté pan over medium-high heat. Add the apple, sugar, and cinnamon and blend well. Cook, stirring occasionally, for 2 to 3 minutes, or until the sugar just starts to caramelize. Remove the pan from the heat and place it on a cooling rack. When the apple mixture is cool, transfer it to the prepared baking sheet and freeze for 1 hour or more.

RECIPE CONTINUES

When you are ready to make the smoothie, place the apple juice, optional honey, apple mixture, and ice cream in a blender and mix by using the on/off pulse function until the ingredients are mostly blended. Continue mixing, gradually increasing the speed, until the mixture is smooth. Pour the smoothie into a glass and garnish with a Cinnamon and Sugar Twist (page 219) or top with Pastry Crunch (page 198), if desired.

Banana and Peanut Butter Obsession

This smoothie, with its sinfully decadent combination of banana, peanut butter, and chocolate-peanut butter ice cream, is outrageously tempting. It is destined to become a favorite, especially if you like peanut butter. In fact, you can add more peanut butter—if you dare.

1 SERVING

½ to ⅔ cup milk

1 cup partially frozen diced banana

⅓ cup or more creamy peanut butter

½ cup chocolate-peanut butter or
favorite chocolate ice cream

Place all the ingredients in a blender and mix by using the on/off pulse function until the ingredients are mostly blended. Continue mixing, gradually increasing the speed, until the mixture is smooth. Pour the smoothie into a glass and garnish with a Peanut Butter–Chocolate Drop (page 227), if desired.

Banana, Raspberry, and Pistachio Addiction

Hats off to the ice cream producers for making pistachio ice cream. Teamed up with banana and raspberry, this addictive creation has *sinful* written all over it.

1 SERVING

⅔ to ¾ cup milk
1 cup partially frozen diced banana
½ cup partially frozen raspberries
¼ cup coarsely chopped Pine Nut Brittle (page 201)
¾ cup pistachio or favorite vanilla ice cream

Place all the ingredients in a blender and mix by using the on/off pulse function until the ingredients are mostly blended. Continue mixing, gradually increasing the speed, until the mixture is smooth. Pour the smoothie into a glass and garnish with a Cinnamon and Sugar Twist (page 219), if desired.

Banana Split Smoothie

There seems to be a "split" over who created the banana split. The people of Wilmington, Ohio, claim that restaurant owner Ernest Hazard created this special sundae during the winter of 1907 in order to attract students from nearby Wilmington College. On the other hand, the folks of Latrobe, Pennsylvania, say that an optometrist named Dr. David Strickler created the banana split at his pharmacy in 1904. Whoever invented it, we can all be grateful for this decadent treat that blends beautifully into a sensually delicious smoothie.

1 SERVING

⅔ to ¾ cup pineapple juice
½ cup partially frozen diced banana
½ cup partially frozen diced pineapple
½ cup partially frozen diced strawberries
½ cup banana split or favorite vanilla ice cream

Place all the ingredients in a blender and mix by using the on/off pulse function until the ingredients are mostly blended. Continue mixing, gradually increasing the speed, until the mixture is smooth. Pour the smoothie into a glass and garnish with a dollop of whipped cream and a cherry, if desired.

Blackberry Pie

Delicately spiced with cinnamon and blended with a rich, creamy vanilla ice cream, this smoothie is the ultimate expression of black-berries. After one taste you'll think you died and went to heaven.

1 SERVING

⅔ to ¾ cup orange juice
1 tablespoon honey, or to taste
1 ½ cups partially frozen blackberries
¼ teaspoon ground cinnamon
½ cup vanilla ice cream

Place all the ingredients in a blender and mix by using the on/off pulse function until the ingredients are mostly blended. Continue mixing, gradually increasing the speed, until the mixture is smooth. Pour the smoothie into a glass and garnish with Berries on a Skewer (page 212) or top with Pastry Crunch (page 198), if desired.

Blueberry and Pineapple Cheesecake

This opulent blueberry, pineapple, and cheese-cake smoothie may be one of the easiest indulgences you've ever prepared.

1 SERVING

⅔ to ¾ cup pineapple juice
1 teaspoon honey, or to taste (optional)
1 cup partially frozen diced pineapple
½ cup partially frozen blueberries
½ cup blueberry cheesecake or
    favorite cheesecake flavor ice cream

Place all the ingredients in a blender and mix by using the on/off pulse function until the ingredients are mostly blended. Continue mixing, gradually increasing the speed, until the mixture is smooth. Pour the smoothie into a glass and garnish with a Pineapple Chip (page 231), if desired.

Blueberry and Pineapple Cobbler

A traditional cobbler is made with fruit and chunks of dough. Some believe the chunks of dough that form the top crust of the dessert resemble the rounded surface of a cobbled road, hence the name *cobbler*. Although this delectable blueberry and pineapple smoothie is made sans dough, you can mimic its dessert cousin by spooning a layer of Pastry Crunch over the finished product.

1 SERVING

⅔ to ¾ cup pineapple juice
2 teaspoons honey, or to taste
1 cup partially frozen blueberries
½ cup partially frozen diced pineapple
¼ teaspoon ground cinnamon
¼ teaspoon ground nutmeg
½ cup vanilla ice cream

Place all the ingredients in a blender and mix by using the on/off pulse function until the ingredients are mostly blended. Continue mixing, gradually increasing the speed, until the mixture is smooth. Pour the smoothie into a glass and top with Pastry Crunch (page 198), if desired.

Blueberry, Blackberry, and Strawberry Cheesecake

You may find it hard to believe that cheesecake is thought to have originated in ancient Greece. The first recorded mention of it is as a treat being served to athletes during the first Olympic games, held in 776 B.C. What's even more amazing is the passion we continue to have for this sensually creamy delight. By combining a rich cheesecake ice cream with a variety of berries, this smoothie will satisfy any craving you may have for something that is sinfully rich.

1 SERVING

⅔ to ¾ cup pineapple juice
½ cup partially frozen blueberries
½ cup partially frozen blackberries
½ cup partially frozen diced strawberries
½ cup blueberry or strawberry cheesecake ice cream

Place all the ingredients in a blender and mix by using the on/off pulse function until the ingredients are mostly blended. Continue mixing, gradually increasing the speed, until the mixture is smooth. Pour the smoothie into a glass and garnish with Berries on a Skewer (page 212) or top with graham cracker crumbs, if desired.

Blueberry Buckle Smoothie

A buckle is a type of cake consisting of a bottom cakelike layer made with blueberries added to the batter and a top layer of streusel topping. Although a buckle may be considered to be a very simple dessert, when its ingredients are combined with apple juice in your blender, it easily morphs into a sensuous blueberry smoothie.

1 SERVING

⅔ to ¾ cup apple juice
1 ½ cups partially frozen blueberries
¼ teaspoon ground cinnamon
⅛ teaspoon ground ginger
⅛ teaspoon ground nutmeg
½ cup lemon custard or favorite vanilla ice cream

Place all the ingredients in a blender and mix by using the on/off pulse function until the ingredients are mostly blended. Continue mixing, gradually increasing the speed, until the mixture is smooth. Pour the smoothie into a glass and top with Pastry Crunch (page 198), if desired.

Caramelized Pineapple with Pralines and Cream Ice Cream

It's well worth the few minutes it takes to broil the pineapple before adding it to this heavenly smoothie. You'll adore the sensational taste of caramelized brown sugar in this tropical delight.

1 SERVING

¼ cup firmly packed dark brown sugar

1 teaspoon ground cinnamon

1 ½ cups cubed pineapple

⅔ to ¾ cup pineapple juice

1 teaspoon honey

½ cup pralines and cream ice cream

Preheat the oven broiler. Line a baking sheet with freezer paper. Set aside.

Combine the brown sugar and cinnamon in a small bowl and blend well. Place the pineapple in a single layer in a broilerproof pan and sprinkle with the brown sugar mixture. Place the pan under the broiler and broil for 3 to 6 minutes, or until the brown sugar just begins to caramelize. Watch carefully to be sure the pineapple doesn't burn. Remove the pan from the oven and place it on a cooling rack.

RECIPE CONTINUES

When the pineapple mixture is cool, transfer it to the prepared baking sheet and freeze for 1 hour or more.

When you are ready to make the smoothie, place the pineapple juice, honey, pineapple mixture, and ice cream in a blender and mix by using the on/off pulse function until the ingredients are mostly blended. Continue mixing, gradually increasing the speed, until the mixture is smooth. Pour the smoothie into a glass and garnish with a Cinnamon-Dipped Tortilla Triangle (page 221), if desired.

Caribbean Coffee Delight

If you're looking for the perfect smoothie to give you a boost, you'll find this coffee-enriched smoothie, combined with banana, spices, and heavenly chocolate ice cream, to be the perfect elixir.

1 SERVING

½ cup chilled espresso or strong coffee
2 to 3 teaspoons honey, or to taste
1 cup partially frozen diced banana
⅛ teaspoon ground cinnamon
⅛ teaspoon ground ginger
⅛ teaspoon ground nutmeg
½ cup chocolate ice cream

Place all the ingredients in a blender and mix by using the on/off pulse function until the ingredients are mostly blended. Continue mixing, gradually increasing the speed, until the mixture is smooth. Pour the smoothie into a glass and garnish with a Cinnamon Pirouette (page 213), if desired.

Cherry Extravaganza

The immediate appeal of this cherry-filled smoothie lies in the ease of its preparation. But don't let its simplicity fool you; this smoothie is a heart-stopping treat. It's bursting with flavors from the delectably sweet cherries and the irresistible ingredients found in the ice cream.

1 SERVING

⅔ to ¾ cup milk
1 ½ cups partially frozen diced cherries
½ cup Dreamery Bing in da Noise or
     favorite cherry and chocolate ice cream

Place all the ingredients in a blender and mix by using the on/off pulse function until the ingredients are mostly blended. Continue mixing, gradually increasing the speed, until the mixture is smooth. Pour the smoothie into a glass and garnish with a Cinnamon and Sugar Twist (page 219), if desired.

Cherry, Green Tea, and Mint Fusion

You might think the unusual ingredients in this smoothie would clash, but instead they harmonize in a subtle way, resulting in a smoothie that is not only sumptuous but healthy because of the addition of green tea, known for its high antioxidant value. Who said if it's good for you it can't taste good!

1 SERVING

3 green tea bags (or 1 tablespoon loose green tea leaves)
3 to 4 large fresh mint leaves
½ cup boiling water
1 cup orange juice
¼ cup sugar
1 teaspoon pure vanilla extract
1 ½ cups cherries, halved
½ cup vanilla ice cream

Place a strainer over a medium bowl. Line a baking sheet with freezer paper. Set aside.

Place the tea bags and mint leaves in a medium bowl. Pour the boiling water over the tea mixture and cover the bowl with plastic wrap. Allow the tea mixture to steep for 2 minutes.

RECIPE CONTINUES

Place the orange juice, sugar, and vanilla in a medium saucepan and bring to a boil over high heat, stirring occasionally to dissolve the sugar. Remove the saucepan from the heat. Strain the tea mixture into the orange juice mixture (discard the tea bags and mint) and blend well. Add the cherries and blend. Allow the mixture to come to room temperature. When the cherry mixture is cool, transfer it to the strainer over the bowl (reserve the liquid). Place the cherries on the prepared baking sheet and freeze for 1 hour or more. Cover the bowl containing the liquid and refrigerate.

When you are ready to make the smoothie, place the reserved cherry mixture liquid, the cherries, and the ice cream in a blender and mix by using the on/off pulse function until the ingredients are mostly blended. Continue mixing, gradually increasing the speed, until the mixture is smooth. Pour the smoothie into a glass and garnish with a Vanilla Pirouette (page 213), if desired.

Chocolate Banana Latte

Caffe latte is traditionally made with espresso coffee and lots of foamy steamed milk. Adding chocolate and banana and replacing the milk with rich ice cream elevates this popular coffee treat to a new dimension.

1 SERVING

½ cup chilled espresso or strong coffee
2 tablespoons Chocolate Syrup (page 191)
1 teaspoon honey
1 cup partially frozen diced banana
¼ teaspoon ground cinnamon
½ cup caramel pecan or favorite vanilla or
    coffee ice cream

Place all the ingredients in a blender and mix by using the on/off pulse function until the ingredients are mostly blended. Continue mixing, gradually increasing the speed, until the mixture is smooth. Pour the smoothie into a glass and garnish with a Chocolate-Dipped Tortilla Triangle (page 221), if desired.

Glazed Strawberry Cheese Rapture

The balsamic vinegar provides a real zip to the strawberries by intensifying their luscious flavor, while the rich and creamy mascarpone cheese complements the fruit in this unusual smoothie.

1 SERVING

1 ½ cups diced strawberries
1 tablespoon good-quality balsamic vinegar
1 tablespoon sugar
⅔ to ¾ cup pineapple juice
½ teaspoon pure vanilla extract
2 tablespoons mascarpone cheese
½ to ¾ cup vanilla bean ice cream

Combine the strawberries, vinegar, and sugar in a medium bowl and stir until well blended. Cover the bowl and place it in the freezer for 2 hours.

When you are ready to make the smoothie, place the pineapple juice, vanilla, strawberry mixture, mascarpone cheese, and ice cream in a blender and mix by using the on/off pulse function until the ingredients are mostly blended. Continue mixing, gradually increasing the speed, until the mixture is smooth. Pour the smoothie into a glass and garnish with a Strawberry Fan (page 233), if desired.

Hot and Spicy Smoothie

Whoever heard of a smoothie made with cayenne pepper? Well, it works in this one. The sweetness of the banana blends sublimely with the spices and ice cream, and the pepper gives it a real kick. The recipe only calls for ⅛ teaspoon cayenne pepper, but if you like fire, feel free to add more.

1 SERVING

½ to ⅔ cup milk
1 cup partially frozen diced banana
¼ teaspoon ground cinnamon
¼ teaspoon ground ginger
⅛ teaspoon ground cardamom
⅛ teaspoon ground nutmeg
⅛ teaspoon cayenne pepper
½ cup vanilla ice cream

Place all the ingredients in a blender and mix by using the on/off pulse function until the ingredients are mostly blended. Continue mixing, gradually increasing the speed, until the mixture is smooth. Pour the smoothie into a glass and garnish with a Cinnamon Wonton Crisp (page 223), if desired.

Indian Pudding Smoothie

New Englanders used to call cornmeal Indian meal, which may explain why the dessert namesake of this smoothie is called Indian pudding. Although this cool refresher is made sans cornmeal, the other traditional Indian pudding ingredients closely mimic the wonderful taste of the original delectable dessert.

1 SERVING

½ to ⅔ cup milk
1 tablespoon molasses
1 tablespoon maple syrup
1 cup partially frozen diced banana
1 tablespoon firmly packed dark brown sugar
¼ teaspoon ground ginger
⅛ teaspoon ground cinnamon
½ cup vanilla ice cream

Place all the ingredients in a blender and mix by using the on/off pulse function until the ingredients are mostly blended. Continue mixing, gradually increasing the speed, until the mixture is smooth. Pour the smoothie into a glass and garnish with a Crisp Banana Wafer (page 225), if desired.

Jitterbug Smoothie

If you're looking for a little spice in your life, then this coffee-and-hazelnut-flavored smoothie is the perfect elixir.

1 SERVING

⅔ cup chilled espresso or strong coffee
1 tablespoon hazelnut-flavored syrup
1 cup partially frozen diced banana
½ cup chocolate ice cream

Place all the ingredients in a blender and mix by using the on/off pulse function until the ingredients are mostly blended. Continue mixing, gradually increasing the speed, until the mixture is smooth. Pour the smoothie into a glass and garnish with a Chocolate-Dipped Frozen Baby Banana (page 217), if desired.

Key Lime, Pineapple, and Banana Enchantment

Originally from Asia, the Key lime is a small, round citrus fruit with a unique bitter tartness that gives it a special taste. Although Key lime juice concentrate is most often used to make a pie, when it's combined with other fruits and ice cream, the end result is a temptingly sweet and tart smoothie.

1 SERVING

⅔ to ¾ cup pineapple juice

2 tablespoons Key lime juice concentrate

1 teaspoon honey, or to taste

1 cup partially frozen diced pineapple

½ cup partially frozen diced banana

½ cup vanilla bean ice cream

Place all the ingredients in a blender and mix by using the on/off pulse function until the ingredients are mostly blended. Continue mixing, gradually increasing the speed, until the mixture is smooth. Pour the smoothie into a glass and garnish with a Pineapple Chip (page 231), if desired.

Lemonberry Tease

This smoothie provides a double dose of berries complemented by tangy lemon custard ice cream. It makes you want to pucker up just thinking about it.

1 SERVING

⅔ to ¾ cup pineapple juice
1 cup partially frozen blueberries
½ cup partially frozen raspberries
½ cup lemon custard ice cream

Place all the ingredients in a blender and mix by using the on/off pulse function until the ingredients are mostly blended. Continue mixing, gradually increasing the speed, until the mixture is smooth. Pour the smoothie into a glass and garnish with a Strawberry Fan (page 233) or top with crushed amaretti cookies, if desired.

Macadamia Banana Infatuation

Sautéing bananas with brown sugar and cinnamon brings out their rich flavor; when you combine them with macadamia brittle ice cream, this smoothie becomes irresistible.

1 SERVING

2 tablespoons (¼ stick) unsalted butter

1 ½ cups diced banana

2 tablespoons firmly packed dark brown sugar

¼ teaspoon ground cinnamon

½ cup milk

1 teaspoon honey, or to taste (optional)

¾ cup macadamia brittle or favorite vanilla ice cream

Line a baking sheet with freezer paper. Set aside.

Melt the butter in a medium sauté pan over medium heat. Add the banana, brown sugar, and cinnamon and blend well. Cook for 6 to 7 minutes, or until the bananas are tender, stirring occasionally. Remove the pan from the heat and place it on a cooling rack. When the banana mixture is cool, transfer it to the prepared baking sheet and freeze for 1 hour or more.

When you are ready to make the smoothie, place the milk, optional honey, banana mixture, and ice cream in a blender and mix by using the on/off pulse function until the ingredients are mostly blended. Continue mixing, gradually increasing the speed, until the mixture is smooth. Pour the smoothie into a glass and garnish with a Cinnamon and Sugar Twist (page 219), if desired.

Macadamia Orange Temptation

This tropical creation is cold, creamy, rich, and impressively delicious.

1 SERVING

²/₃ to ³/₄ cup orange juice
1 teaspoon honey, or to taste
1 cup partially frozen diced orange
½ cup partially frozen diced banana
½ cup macadamia brittle or favorite vanilla ice cream

Place all the ingredients in a blender and mix by using the on/off pulse function until the ingredients are mostly blended. Continue mixing, gradually increasing the speed, until the mixture is smooth. Pour the smoothie into a glass and garnish with a Crisp Banana Wafer (page 225), if desired.

Peach and Blueberry Cobbler

You'll want to dive right into this summery smoothie, replete with peaches and blueberries and kicked up a notch with just the right amount of cobbler spices.

1 SERVING

⅔ to ¾ cup peach nectar
1 cup partially frozen diced peach
½ cup partially frozen blueberries
½ teaspoon ground cinnamon
¼ teaspoon ground nutmeg
Dash of coarsely ground pepper
½ cup pralines and cream or
   favorite vanilla ice cream

Place all the ingredients in a blender and mix by using the on/off pulse function until the ingredients are mostly blended. Continue mixing, gradually increasing the speed, until the mixture is smooth. Pour the smoothie into a glass and top with Pastry Crunch (page 198), if desired.

Peach and Butterscotch Sundae Smoothie

The simplicity of the ingredients belies the rich taste of this smoothie. Peaches and Butterscotch Sauce meld together into an incredibly delectable pleasure in a glass.

1 SERVING

⅔ to ¾ cup peach nectar
3 tablespoons Butterscotch Sauce (page 181)
1 ½ cups partially frozen diced peach
½ cup peach or favorite vanilla ice cream

Place all the ingredients in a blender and mix by using the on/off pulse function until the ingredients are mostly blended. Continue mixing, gradually increasing the speed, until the mixture is smooth. Pour the smoothie into a glass and garnish with a Cinnamon Wonton Crisp (page 223), if desired.

Peach and Caramel Celebration

This smoothie is about succulent peaches, creamy caramel, and soul-stirring ice cream spun together into an unforgettable treat.

1 SERVING

⅔ to ¾ cup peach nectar

3 tablespoons Caramel Sauce (page 182)

1 ½ cups partially frozen diced peach

½ cup pralines and cream ice cream

Place all the ingredients in a blender and mix by using the on/off pulse function until the ingredients are mostly blended. Continue mixing, gradually increasing the speed, until the mixture is smooth. Pour the smoothie into a glass and garnish with a Vanilla Pirouette (page 213), if desired.

Peach and Raspberry Melba

Peach Melba is a dessert created in the late 1800s by the famous French chef Escoffier for Dame Nellie Melba, a popular Australian opera singer. It is traditionally made with peaches and a raspberry sauce, and these fruits are a perfect match when combined into a sensuously rich smoothie.

1 SERVING

²⁄₃ to ¾ cup peach nectar
1 cup partially frozen diced peach
½ cup partially frozen raspberries
½ cup raspberry gelato or favorite strawberry,
    raspberry, or vanilla ice cream
1 to 2 teaspoons Raspberry Sauce (page 204) (optional)

Place the peach nectar, peach, raspberries, and gelato in a blender and mix by using the on/off pulse function until the ingredients are mostly blended. Continue mixing, gradually increasing the speed, until the mixture is smooth. Spoon the Raspberry Sauce, if using, in the bottom of a glass and add the smoothie. Garnish with Berries on a Skewer (page 212) or top with crumbled amaretti cookies, if desired.

Peach and Raspberry Transgression

This smoothie is a stunning combination of ethereal ingredients: raspberries, peach, and heavenly pistachio ice cream. Enjoy this smoothie as a naughty midday indulgence or accompanied by a tray of miniature sweets as a light dessert after dinner.

1 SERVING

⅔ to ¾ cup peach nectar
3 tablespoons Raspberry Sauce (page 204)
1 cup partially frozen diced peach
½ cup partially frozen raspberries
½ cup pistachio or favorite vanilla ice cream

Place all the ingredients in a blender and mix by using the on/off pulse function until the ingredients are mostly blended. Continue mixing, gradually increasing the speed, until the mixture is smooth. Pour the smoothie into a glass and garnish with a Cinnamon Pirouette (page 213), if desired.

Peach, Mango, and Strawberry Cobbler

Basic ingredients merge to create an absolutely delicious smoothie. It is certain to become a staple in your smoothie repertoire.

1 SERVING

⅔ to ¾ cup peach nectar
1 teaspoon honey, or to taste (optional)
½ cup partially frozen diced peach
½ cup partially frozen diced mango
½ cup partially frozen diced strawberries
½ cup vanilla ice cream

Place all the ingredients in a blender and mix by using the on/off pulse function until the ingredients are mostly blended. Continue mixing, gradually increasing the speed, until the mixture is smooth. Pour the smoothie into a glass and top with Pastry Crunch (page 198), if desired.

Peanut Butter and Jelly Smoothie

According to food historians, both peanut butter and jelly were part of U.S. military rations during World War II. It's believed that American GIs may have added jelly to the peanut butter to make it easier to eat, thus inventing the classic American sandwich, a PB & J. Had the blender been available, they might have discovered, as we have, this novel peanut butter and jelly smoothie.

1 SERVING

½ to ⅔ cup milk
1 cup partially frozen diced banana
¼ cup or more creamy peanut butter
3 to 4 tablespoons strawberry preserves
½ cup vanilla ice cream

Place all the ingredients in a blender and mix by using the on/off pulse function until the ingredients are mostly blended. Continue mixing, gradually increasing the speed, until the mixture is smooth. Pour the smoothie into a glass and garnish with a Strawberry Fan (page 233), if desired.

Pineapple Bewitchery

The only magic you'll need to make this savory smoothie is a pot and some sugar and spices to cook up the gingery brew used to flavor the pineapple.

1 SERVING

½ cup cold water
¼ cup sugar
2 pieces of fresh ginger,
    peeled and cut ¼ inch thick
1 3-inch cinnamon stick
1 ½ cups cubed pineapple
⅔ to ¾ cup pineapple juice
½ cup pralines and cream or
    favorite vanilla ice cream

Place a strainer over a medium bowl. Line a baking sheet with freezer paper. Set aside.

Combine the water, sugar, ginger, and cinnamon stick in a medium saucepan over medium-high heat and bring to a boil, stirring occasionally to dissolve the sugar. Lower the heat to medium, cover, and simmer for 10 minutes. Add the pineapple and blend well. Simmer for 5 minutes, stirring occasionally. Remove the saucepan from the heat and allow the pineapple mixture to come to room temperature. When the pineapple mixture is cool, transfer it to the strainer over the bowl (discard the liquid and cinnamon stick). Place the pineapple on the pre-pared baking sheet and freeze for 1 hour or more.

When you are ready to make the smoothie, place the pineapple juice, pineapple, and ice cream in a blender and mix by using the on/off pulse func-tion until the ingredients are mostly blended. Con-tinue mixing, gradually increasing the speed, until the mixture is smooth. Pour the smoothie into a glass and garnish with a Pineapple Chip (page 231), if desired.

Pineapple, Blueberry, and Banana Illusion

It's almost unreal how sensational this fruit-filled smoothie tastes—maybe it's the macadamia brittle ice cream that adds the seductive flavor.

1 SERVING

⅔ to ¾ cup pineapple juice
2 teaspoons honey, or to taste
½ cup partially frozen diced pineapple
½ cup partially frozen blueberries
½ cup partially frozen diced banana
½ cup macadamia brittle or
    favorite vanilla ice cream

Place all the ingredients in a blender and mix by using the on/off pulse function until the ingredients are mostly blended. Continue mixing, gradually increasing the speed, until the mixture is smooth. Pour the smoothie into a glass and garnish with a Pineapple Chip (page 231), if desired.

Pineapple Cobbler

I like this intriguing mixture of pineapple and spices blended with a rich and creamy vanilla bean ice cream. To finish it off, top with a layer of delicious Pastry Crunch.

1 SERVING

⅔ to ¾ cup pineapple juice
1 ½ cups partially frozen diced pineapple
¼ teaspoon ground cinnamon
⅛ teaspoon ground nutmeg
½ cup vanilla bean ice cream

Place all the ingredients in a blender and mix by using the on/off pulse function until the ingredients are mostly blended. Continue mixing, gradually increasing the speed, until the mixture is smooth. Pour the smoothie into a glass and top with Pastry Crunch (page 198), if desired.

Pineapple-Mango Breeze

What could be better than to indulge in a smoothie made with pineapple, mango, banana, and rum raisin ice cream? You'll be easily seduced by its delectable, tropical flavors.

1 SERVING

⅔ to ¾ cup pineapple juice
½ cup partially frozen diced pineapple
½ cup partially frozen diced mango
½ cup partially frozen diced banana
½ cup rum raisin or favorite vanilla ice cream

Place all the ingredients in a blender and mix by using the on/off pulse function until the ingredients are mostly blended. Continue mixing, gradually increasing the speed, until the mixture is smooth. Pour the smoothie into a glass and garnish with a Cinnamon and Sugar Twist (page 219), if desired.

Pineapple, Strawberry, and Pistachio Temptation

This smoothie is a celebration of fruity flavors, enhanced by the addition of a sensational pistachio ice cream.

1 SERVING

⅔ to ¾ cup pineapple juice
1 cup partially frozen diced pineapple
½ cup partially frozen diced strawberries
½ cup pistachio or favorite vanilla ice cream

Place all the ingredients in a blender and mix by using the on/off pulse function until the ingredients are mostly blended. Continue mixing, gradually increasing the speed, until the mixture is smooth. Pour the smoothie into a glass and garnish with a Strawberry Fan (page 233) or top with crumbled amaretti cookies, if desired.

Pineapple Upside-Down Cake

The classic American pineapple upside-down cake originated sometime after 1903, when Jim Dole introduced canned pineapple. Twenty-two years later, in 1925, the Hawaiian Pineapple Company (now Dole Pineapple) held a pineapple recipe contest, and twenty-five hundred of the more than sixty thousand recipes submitted were for a variety of pineapple upside-down cake. Now in the twenty-first century, we can enjoy recipe #2501 in the form of this delightful treat blended into a sensational smoothie.

1 SERVING

1 tablespoon unsalted butter, melted
¼ cup firmly packed light brown sugar
1 ½ cups diced pineapple
⅔ to ¾ cup pineapple juice
½ cup vanilla bean ice cream

Place a strainer over a medium bowl. Line a baking sheet with freezer paper. Set aside.

Melt the butter in a medium sauté pan over medium heat. Swirl the pan to coat evenly. Add the brown sugar and blend well. Increase the heat to medium-high and cook the mixture until it begins to bubble. Add the pineapple and pineapple juice and blend well. Bring the mixture to a boil, stirring occasionally. Remove the pan from the heat and place it on a cooling rack. When the pineapple mixture is cool, transfer it to the strainer over the bowl (reserve the liquid). Place the pineapple on the prepared baking sheet and freeze for 1 hour or more. Cover the bowl containing the liquid and refrigerate.

When you are ready to make the smoothie, place the reserved liquid, pineapple, and ice cream in a blender and mix by using the on/off pulse function until the ingredients are mostly blended. Continue mixing, gradually increasing the speed, until the mixture is smooth. Pour the smoothie into a glass and garnish with a Pineapple Chip (page 231), if desired.

Pine Nut Pear-adise

The incongruous ingredients that go into this smoothie make it all the more temptingly seductive to try. If you decide not to include the Pine Nut Brittle, the smoothie still remains a deliciously satisfying treat.

1 SERVING

⅔ to ¾ cup pineapple juice
1 cup partially frozen diced pear
½ cup partially frozen diced banana
2 tablespoons coarsely chopped Pine Nut Brittle
   (page 201)
½ cup Almond Joy or favorite coconut or
   vanilla ice cream

Place all the ingredients in a blender and mix by using the on/off pulse function until the ingredients are mostly blended. Continue mixing, gradually increasing the speed, until the mixture is smooth. Pour the smoothie into a glass and garnish with a Pear Chip (page 229), if desired.

Pumpkin Pie

Pumpkin pie is traditionally served during wintry holiday times, but you can get the same festive feeling when you whip up a glassful of this comfort smoothie made with the traditional ingredients used to make this baker's delight.

1 SERVING

½ cup orange juice or milk
⅛ teaspoon pure vanilla extract
¾ cup partially frozen diced orange
½ cup chilled solid-pack pumpkin
2 tablespoons firmly packed dark brown sugar
¼ teaspoon ground cinnamon
⅛ teaspoon ground ginger
¾ cup vanilla ice cream

Place all the ingredients in a blender and mix by using the on/off pulse function until the ingredients are mostly blended. Continue mixing, gradually increasing the speed, until the mixture is smooth. Pour the smoothie into a glass and top with Pastry Crunch (page 198) or graham cracker crumbs, if desired.

Raspberry Clementine Euphoria

This extravagant smoothie made with Godiva ice cream is the very definition of *sinful*. Treat yourself and splurge on this raspberry and clementine treat.

1 SERVING

⅔ to ¾ cup milk

1 teaspoon honey, or to taste

1 cup partially frozen diced clementines

½ cup partially frozen raspberries

½ cup Godiva White Chocolate Raspberry or
     favorite vanilla or white chocolate ice cream

Place all the ingredients in a blender and mix by using the on/off pulse function until the ingredients are mostly blended. Continue mixing, gradually increasing the speed, until the mixture is smooth. Pour the smoothie into a glass and garnish with Berries on a Skewer (page 212), if desired.

Razzle~Dazzle Raspberry, Blueberry, and Strawberry Smoothie

Enjoy this berry-filled smoothie as an afternoon indulgence or serve it as a light dessert after an elegant meal.

1 SERVING

⅔ to ¾ cup pineapple juice

2 tablespoons Raspberry Sauce (page 204)

½ cup partially frozen raspberries

½ cup partially frozen blueberries

½ cup partially frozen diced strawberries

⅔ cup raspberry gelato or favorite strawberry, raspberry, or vanilla ice cream

Place all the ingredients in a blender and mix by using the on/off pulse function until the ingredients are mostly blended. Continue mixing, gradually increasing the speed, until the mixture is smooth. Pour the smoothie into a glass and garnish with a Strawberry Fan (page 233), if desired.

Red-Hot Banana Smoothie

Your eyes are not deceiving you. This smoothie is made with real hot pepper sauce. You'll adore the balance of sweetness from the fruit and ice cream and the intense heat from the sauce.

1 SERVING

⅔ cup pineapple juice
½ teaspoon or more Tabasco sauce or
    favorite hot pepper sauce
1 cup partially frozen diced banana
½ cup vanilla ice cream

Place all the ingredients in a blender and mix by using the on/off pulse function until the ingredients are mostly blended. Continue mixing, gradually increasing the speed, until the mixture is smooth. Pour the smoothie into a glass and garnish with a Cinnamon Wonton Crisp (page 223), if desired.

South-of-the-Border Smoothie Sensation

If your tastes lean toward the flavors of south-western cuisine, then you'll be pleased with this smoothie made with a blend of luscious fruits spiced up with a hint of cinnamon.

1 SERVING

⅔ to ¾ cup orange juice
¼ cup firmly packed dark brown sugar
¼ teaspoon ground cinnamon
½ cup partially frozen diced mango
½ cup partially frozen diced banana
½ cup partially frozen diced pineapple
½ cup macadamia brittle or favorite vanilla ice cream

Combine the orange juice, brown sugar, and cinnamon in a small saucepan over medium-low heat for 5 minutes, stirring frequently to dissolve the sugar. Increase the heat to medium-high and boil for 5 minutes. Remove the saucepan from the heat and allow the orange juice mixture to come to room temperature. When the orange juice mixture is cool, transfer it to a covered container and refrigerate for 30 minutes, or until it is well chilled.

When you are ready to make the smoothie, place the orange juice mixture, mango, banana,

RECIPE CONTINUES

pineapple, and ice cream in a blender and mix by using the on/off pulse function until the ingredients are mostly blended. Continue mixing, gradually increasing the speed, until the mixture is smooth. Pour the smoothie into a glass and garnish with a Cinnamon-Dipped Tortilla Triangle (page 221), if desired.

Spiced Apple and Caramel Smoothie

To be certain you always have a ready supply of this delicious apple mixture, make a large quantity, then divide it into the portions needed to make one smoothie and place each one in a freezer bag. The mixture will keep for four to six weeks.

1 SERVING

2 tablespoons (¼ stick) unsalted butter, melted
⅔ to ¾ cup apple juice
2 tablespoons firmly packed light brown sugar
1 2-inch cinnamon stick
½ teaspoon black peppercorns
1 whole star anise
1 ½ cups peeled and diced Golden Delicious apples
½ cup caramel or favorite vanilla ice cream

Preheat the oven to 400°F. Lightly coat a glass baking dish (such as a 9-inch pie plate) with a nonstick vegetable spray. Line a baking sheet with freezer paper. Set aside.

Combine the butter, 2 tablespoons apple juice, brown sugar, cinnamon stick, peppercorns, and star anise in a medium bowl and blend well. Add the apples and toss to coat all over. Transfer the apple

RECIPE CONTINUES

mixture to the prepared baking dish and bake for 30 minutes, or until the apples are tender, stirring occasionally. Remove the dish from the oven and place it on a cooling rack. When the apple mixture is cool (remove and discard the spices), transfer it to the prepared baking sheet and freeze for 1 hour or more.

When you are ready to make the smoothie, place the remaining 8 to 10 tablespoons apple juice, the apple mixture, and ice cream in a blender and mix by using the on/off pulse function until the ingredients are mostly blended. Continue mixing, gradually increasing the speed, until the mixture is smooth. Pour the smoothie into a glass and garnish with an Apple Chip (page 210), if desired.

Spumoni

Although spumoni is traditionally made with cherry, chocolate, and pistachio ice creams, I think you'll agree that this smoothie doesn't require any chocolate to improve its taste. On the other hand, feel free to add some chocolate ice cream or sauce—it can't hurt.

1 SERVING

²/₃ to ³/₄ cup milk
1 ½ cups partially frozen diced strawberries
¼ cup diced candied cherries
³/₄ to 1 cup pistachio or vanilla ice cream

Place all the ingredients in a blender and mix by using the on/off pulse function until the ingredients are mostly blended. Continue mixing, gradually increasing the speed, until the mixture is smooth. Pour the smoothie into a glass and garnish with a Strawberry Fan (page 233), if desired.

Strawberries and Cream

It takes only minutes to prepare this seductively delicious strawberry smoothie. Enjoy!

1 SERVING

⅔ to ¾ cup apple juice
1 teaspoon honey, or to taste
1 ½ cups partially frozen diced strawberries
½ cup strawberry ice cream

Place all the ingredients in a blender and mix by using the on/off pulse function until the ingredients are mostly blended. Continue mixing, gradually increasing the speed, until the mixture is smooth. Pour the smoothie into a glass and garnish with a Strawberry Fan (page 233), if desired.

Strawberry Cheesecake

Do you ever crave a piece of dense cheesecake smothered in strawberries, but don't have the time or energy to pick up a slice from your favorite deli? Now you can have it anytime you want by keeping your freezer and refrigerator stocked with the simple ingredients found in this smoothie.

1 SERVING

⅔ to ¾ cup milk
1 teaspoon honey, or to taste (optional)
1 cup partially frozen diced strawberries
½ cup partially frozen diced banana
½ cup strawberry cheesecake or
    favorite cheesecake flavor ice cream

Place all the ingredients in a blender and mix by using the on/off pulse function until the ingredients are mostly blended. Continue mixing, gradually increasing the speed, until the mixture is smooth. Pour the smoothie into a glass and garnish with a Strawberry Fan (page 233), if desired.

Strawberry and Pineapple Colada

Pineapple coladas are all the rage, but imagine your delight when strawberries are added and the combination is whirled into a sumptuous smoothie. It takes this popular combination to new heights.

1 SERVING

⅔ to ¾ cup pineapple juice

1 teaspoon honey, or to taste

¾ cup partially frozen diced strawberries

¾ cup partially frozen diced pineapple

½ cup coconut gelato or favorite coconut or
vanilla ice cream

Place all the ingredients in a blender and mix by using the on/off pulse function until the ingredients are mostly blended. Continue mixing, gradually increasing the speed, until the mixture is smooth. Pour the smoothie into a glass and garnish with a Pineapple Chip (page 231), if desired.

Tropical Fruit with Coconut Gelato

Pairing fruits of the tropics with a rich and creamy coconut gelato is an ethereal experience. Who needs to travel to an island when you can create a South Pacific enjoyment in your own kitchen?

1 SERVING

⅔ to ¾ cup mango nectar or pineapple juice

1 teaspoon honey, or to taste (optional)

½ cup partially frozen diced mango or papaya

½ cup partially frozen diced pineapple

½ cup partially frozen diced banana

½ cup coconut gelato or favorite coconut or
   vanilla ice cream

Place all the ingredients in a blender and mix by using the on/off pulse function until the ingredients are mostly blended. Continue mixing, gradually increasing the speed, until the mixture is smooth. Pour the smoothie into a glass and garnish with a Crisp Banana Wafer (page 225), if desired.

Tutti-Frutti Smoothie

Tutti-frutti is an Italian term used to describe ice cream or other desserts that contain a variety of minced, candied fruits. You'll adore the pleasingly sweet flavor the candied cherries contribute to this pineapple and orange smoothie.

1 SERVING

⅔ to ¾ cup pineapple juice
½ cup partially frozen diced orange
½ cup partially frozen diced pineapple
½ cup diced candied cherries
½ cup vanilla ice cream

Place all the ingredients in a blender and mix by using the on/off pulse function until the ingredients are mostly blended. Continue mixing, gradually increasing the speed, until the mixture is smooth. Pour the smoothie into a glass and garnish with a Pineapple Chip (page 231), if desired.

4

Ultimate Indulgences

Make Mine Thick and Rich

The world loves a spice of wickedness.

—Henry Wadsworth Longfellow
(1807–1882)

IF YOU'RE A SMOOTHIE LOVER AND ALSO LOOK-
ing for a way to add a touch of culinary wickedness
to your life, then get ready to taste some heart-
stopping glassfuls of sinful delights. Whether you
obsess over sensuous chocolate creations, hunger for
peanut butter, or dream about an extraordinarily
rich and creamy ice cream, you are destined to drool
over the utterly indulgent smoothies featured in this
chapter of endless pleasures and satisfaction. These
heavenly treats are made with seductively unforgettable ingredients. Here you'll find Peach and Praline
Indulgence, a peach smoothie made with sinfully
rich Godiva Vanilla Caramel Pecan ice cream and
drop-dead Praline Sauce, as well as Mango and
Macadamia Nut Enchantment, a mango smoothie

featuring luscious Macadamia Nut Praline Crunch and a heavenly caramel sauce.

None of the smoothies found in this chapter are for the faint of heart. They are intended to break down your defenses with such temptations as peanut butter and caramel, and then chocolatize you into submission. After one taste, there's no turning back. You'll have no choice but to finish each one down to the last strawful. With more than forty mouth-watering smoothies to choose from, you'll be counting the hours until you can sample another one. But wait, this book is called *Sinful Smoothies*, so who says you have to watch the clock? Just raise your glass and say, "The devil made me do it!"

Almond Joy Smoothie

The Almond Joy candy bar, introduced in 1947, remains popular to this day, and for good reason. Who could resist such deliriously enticing ingredients as almonds, coconut, and milk chocolate? Fortunately, many ice cream parlors have used these very components to create a sinfully rich ice cream, and when this frozen ambrosia is melded with milk, banana, and chocolate fudge, you end up with an irresistible Almond Joy Smoothie sensation.

1 SERVING

⅔ to ¾ cup milk
2 tablespoons Milk Chocolate Sauce (page 197)
1 cup partially frozen diced banana
½ cup Almond Joy or favorite coconut or
   vanilla ice cream

Place all the ingredients in a blender and mix by using the on/off pulse function until the ingredients are mostly blended. Continue mixing, gradually increasing the speed, until the mixture is smooth. Pour the smoothie into a glass and garnish with a Chocolate-Dipped Frozen Baby Banana (page 217), if desired.

Apricot, Caramel, and Praline Exhilaration

Imagine the ecstasy after taking a sip of this mouthwatering smoothie, made with such ethereal ingredients as juicy apricots, caramel, pecan pralines, and pralines and cream ice cream. It's a celebration!

1 SERVING

⅔ to ¾ cup apricot nectar
2 tablespoons Caramel Sauce (page 182)
1 ½ cups partially frozen diced apricots
2 tablespoons coarsely chopped
    Pecan Praline Crunch (page 199)
½ cup pralines and cream ice cream

Place all the ingredients in a blender and mix by using the on/off pulse function until the ingredients are mostly blended. Continue mixing, gradually increasing the speed, until the mixture is smooth. Pour the smoothie into a glass and garnish with a Cinnamon Wonton Crisp (page 223), if desired.

Baked Apple Pie Smoothie

How could it possibly be sinful to indulge in something as down-home as a Baked Apple Pie Smoothie? You'll be pleased both at how easy it is to assemble the apples before they are baked and with the resulting rich flavor the apples acquire as a result of this extra step.

1 SERVING

2 tablespoons firmly packed dark brown sugar

½ teaspoon ground cinnamon

⅛ teaspoon ground nutmeg

⅛ teaspoon ground cloves

2 large apples, preferably McIntosh, peeled

1 tablespoon butter, cut into 2 pats

2 tablespoons maple syrup

1 cup apple juice

½ cup apple pie or favorite vanilla ice cream

Preheat the oven to 400°F. Line a shallow bowl with nonstick aluminum foil. Set aside.

Combine the brown sugar, cinnamon, nutmeg, and cloves in a small bowl and blend well.

Remove the stems from the top of each apple. Using an apple corer, remove the cores, but do not cut through the bottoms. Place the apples in a baking dish. Fill each hole with the brown sugar mixture and butter, dividing evenly. Spoon the maple

RECIPE CONTINUES

syrup on top. Pour ¼ of the cup apple juice into the baking dish. Bake the apples for 30 to 35 minutes, or until tender, basting the apples every 5 to 8 minutes. Remove the baking dish from the oven and place it on a cooling rack. Allow the baked apples and juice to come to room temperature. When the baked apples and juice are cool, place them in the prepared bowl and freeze for 1 hour or more.

When you are ready to make the smoothie, place the remaining ¾ cup apple juice, the baked apples and juice, and ice cream in a blender and mix by using the on/off pulse function until the ingredients are mostly blended. Continue mixing, gradually increasing the speed, until the mixture is smooth. Pour the smoothie into a glass and garnish with a Cinnamon Pirouette (page 213), if desired.

Banana and Caramel Bliss

This extraordinarily rich smoothie, a wonderful mouthful of creamy delight, is easy to prepare.

1 SERVING

½ to ⅔ cup milk
1 cup partially frozen diced banana
3 tablespoons Caramel Sauce (page 182)
½ cup Dreamery Caramel Toffee Bar Heaven or
    favorite toffee or vanilla ice cream

Place all the ingredients in a blender and mix by using the on/off pulse function until the ingredients are mostly blended. Continue mixing, gradually increasing the speed, until the mixture is smooth. Pour the smoothie into a glass and garnish with a Turtle on a Skewer (page 234), if desired.

Banana and Macadamia Praline Seduction

Let your senses luxuriate in the seductive flavors of this smoothie, which is rich enough to
be enjoyed as an after-dinner dessert or sinful
enough to share with someone special.

1 SERVING

½ to ⅔ cup milk

2 tablespoons Chocolate Sauce (page 190)

1 cup partially frozen diced banana

2 tablespoons coarsely chopped Macadamia Nut
    Praline Crunch (page 193)

½ cup Almond Joy or favorite coconut or
    vanilla ice cream

Place all the ingredients in a blender and mix by
using the on/off pulse function until the ingredients
are mostly blended. Continue mixing, gradually
increasing the speed, until the mixture is smooth.
Pour the smoothie into a glass and garnish with a
Chocolate-Dipped Frozen Baby Banana (page 217),
if desired.

Banana, Butterscotch, and Macadamia Nut Supreme

The next time you're in the mood for a sinfully rich treat, try this combination of decadent ingredients whirled into a devilish treat.

1 SERVING

½ to ⅔ cup milk

3 tablespoons Butterscotch Sauce (page 181)

1 cup partially frozen diced banana

2 tablespoons coarsely chopped Macadamia Nut
    Praline Crunch (page 193)

½ cup macadamia brittle or favorite vanilla ice cream

Place all the ingredients in a blender and mix by using the on/off pulse function until the ingredients are mostly blended. Continue mixing, gradually increasing the speed, until the mixture is smooth. Pour the smoothie into a glass and garnish with a Cinnamon and Sugar Twist (page 219) or top with crushed amaretti cookies, if desired.

Banana, Caramel, and Chocolate Debauchery

How naughty could one get? Well, just try banana, caramel sauce, chocolate-covered peanuts, and chocolate ice cream spun together into a mouthwatering celebration and find out for yourself.

1 SERVING

½ to ⅔ cup milk
2 tablespoons Caramel Sauce (page 182)
1 cup partially frozen diced banana
½ cup chopped chocolate-covered peanuts
½ cup chocolate ice cream

Place all the ingredients in a blender and mix by using the on/off pulse function until the ingredients are mostly blended. Continue mixing, gradually increasing the speed, until the mixture is smooth. Pour the smoothie into a glass and garnish with a Chocolate-Dipped Tortilla Triangle (page 221), if desired.

Banana, Caramel, Milk Chocolate, and Peanut Crunch Fantasy

Simply delicious, this smoothie combines two heavenly sauces (banana and Milk Chocolate and Peanut Crunch) and ice cream—and the blend is perfection.

1 SERVING

½ to ⅔ cup milk
2 tablespoons Milk Chocolate Sauce (page 197)
2 tablespoons Caramel Sauce (page 182)
1 cup partially frozen diced banana
¼ cup Milk Chocolate and Peanut Crunch (page 195)
½ cup vanilla ice cream

Place all the ingredients in a blender and mix by using the on/off pulse function until the ingredients are mostly blended. Continue mixing, gradually increasing the speed, until the mixture is smooth. Pour the smoothie into a glass and garnish with a Turtle on a Skewer (page 234), if desired.

Banana, Hot Fudge, and Caramel Passion

It doesn't get much better than indulging in a combination of banana, hot fudge sauce, and caramel toffee ice cream. The turtle garnish isn't bad, either!

1 SERVING

1 tablespoon unsalted butter

1 ½ cups diced banana

1 tablespoon firmly packed light brown sugar

½ cup milk

1 tablespoon honey, or to taste (optional)

2 to 3 tablespoons Sugar's Hot Fudge Sauce
(page 206)

½ cup Dreamery Caramel Toffee Bar Heaven or
favorite toffee ice cream

Line a baking sheet with freezer paper. Set aside.

Melt the butter in a medium sauté pan over medium-high heat. Add the banana and brown sugar and blend well. Cook, stirring occasionally, for 3 to 4 minutes, or until the banana is tender. Remove the pan from the heat and place it on a cooling rack. When the banana mixture is cool, transfer it to the prepared baking sheet and freeze for 1 hour or more.

When you are ready to make the smoothie, place the milk, optional honey, hot fudge sauce, banana mixture, and ice cream in a blender and mix by using the on/off pulse function until the ingredients are mostly blended. Continue mixing, gradually increasing the speed, until the mixture is smooth. Pour the smoothie into a glass and garnish with a Turtle on a Skewer (page 234), if desired.

Banana, Peanut Butter, and Chocolate Ecstasy

No doubt about it: Chocolate and peanut butter rule in this seductive smoothie. Serve this delectable smoothie as an over-the-top dessert or midday indulgence when you have a craving for something naughty.

1 SERVING

½ to ⅔ cup milk

2 tablespoons Chocolate, Caramel, and Peanut Butter Sauce (page 184)

¼ cup creamy peanut butter

1 cup partially frozen diced banana

½ cup chocolate–peanut butter cup or favorite chocolate ice cream

Place all the ingredients in a blender and mix by using the on/off pulse function until the ingredients are mostly blended. Continue mixing, gradually increasing the speed, until the mixture is smooth. Pour the smoothie into a glass and garnish with a Peanut Butter–Chocolate Drop (page 227), if desired.

Banana, Peanut Butter, and Milk Chocolate Explosion

When you need a chocolate and peanut butter fix right now, you'll be pleased to know that it takes just a few minutes to whip up this sensational smoothie.

1 SERVING

½ to ⅔ cup milk

¼ cup creamy peanut butter

¼ cup Milk Chocolate and Peanut Crunch (page 195)

1 cup partially frozen diced banana

½ cup chocolate or
    favorite chocolate-peanut butter cup ice cream

Place all the ingredients in a blender and mix by using the on/off pulse function until the ingredients are mostly blended. Continue mixing, gradually increasing the speed, until the mixture is smooth. Pour the smoothie into a glass and garnish with a Peanut Butter–Chocolate Drop (page 227), if desired.

Berries and Caramel Mania

This smoothie is a tribute to berries, not only because they are delicious to eat, but also because they're good for you. With the addition of caramel sauce and pralines and cream ice cream, this delectable treat achieves five-star status.

1 SERVING

⅔ to ¾ cup pineapple juice
3 tablespoons Caramel Sauce (page 182)
½ cup partially frozen diced strawberries
½ cup partially frozen blueberries
½ cup partially frozen raspberries
½ cup pralines and cream ice cream

Place all the ingredients in a blender and mix by using the on/off pulse function until the ingredients are mostly blended. Continue mixing, gradually increasing the speed, until the mixture is smooth. Pour the smoothie into a glass and garnish with Berries on a Skewer (page 212), if desired.

Blueberry and Praline Smoothie

The origin of pralines dates back to eighteenth-century France when a chef employed by the French marshal and diplomat Cesar du Plessis-Praslin (pronounced PRAH-lin) created a recipe for coating almonds in sugar. The confection was named after Marshal Praslin, and his chef has been all but forgotten. In New Orleans, pralines are made with pecans. After one taste of this sensational smoothie, I think you'll agree with me that pralines and blueberries are a perfect match.

1 SERVING

⅔ to ¾ cup milk
2 to 3 tablespoons Caramel Sauce (page 182)
1 ½ cups partially frozen blueberries
½ cup pralines and cream ice cream

Place all the ingredients in a blender and mix by using the on/off pulse function until the ingredients are mostly blended. Continue mixing, gradually increasing the speed, until the mixture is smooth. Pour the smoothie into a glass and garnish with Berries on a Skewer (page 212), if desired.

Caffè Speciale

It's no surprise that this smoothie is called *speciale*. The cinnamon and nutmeg give the banana and coffee smoothie a sensuously spicy flavor, while the chocolate adds the pièce de résistance.

1 SERVING

½ cup chilled espresso or strong coffee
1 tablespoon Sugar's Hot Fudge Sauce (page 206)
1 cup partially frozen diced banana
¼ teaspoon ground cinnamon
¼ teaspoon ground nutmeg
½ cup coffee ice cream

Place all the ingredients in a blender and mix by using the on/off pulse function until the ingredients are mostly blended. Continue mixing, gradually increasing the speed, until the mixture is smooth. Pour the smoothie into a glass and garnish with a Chocolate-Dipped Tortilla Triangle (page 221), if desired.

Cajeta Smoothie

Cajeta is a thick, dark syrup made from caramelized sugar and milk—most often goat's milk—and is used in Mexico and in some South American countries as a dessert or as a topping for ice cream or fruit. The caramel sauce used in this smoothie is not as rich as *cajeta* but mimics its intensely rich flavor when blended with the other ingredients.

1 SERVING

½ to ⅔ cup milk
1 cup partially frozen diced banana
3 tablespoons Caramel Sauce (page 182)
½ cup caramel or favorite vanilla or
    pralines and cream ice cream

Place all the ingredients in a blender and mix by using the on/off pulse function until the ingredients are mostly blended. Continue mixing, gradually increasing the speed, until the mixture is smooth. Pour the smoothie into a glass and garnish with a Cinnamon Wonton Crisp (page 223), if desired.

Caramel Apple Pie Smoothie

This mouthwatering smoothie offers a layering of traditional apple pie ingredients with a heavenly Caramel Sauce and vanilla ice cream. Top it off with Pastry Crunch, and you have a lustrous dessert in a glass.

1 SERVING

⅔ to ¾ cup apple juice
1 ½ cups partially frozen diced apple
3 tablespoons Caramel Sauce (page 182)
½ teaspoon ground cinnamon
¼ teaspoon ground ginger
⅛ teaspoon ground nutmeg
½ cup vanilla ice cream
2 tablespoons Pastry Crunch (page 198)

Place the apple juice, apple, Caramel Sauce, cinnamon, ginger, nutmeg, and ice cream in a blender and mix by using the on/off pulse function until the ingredients are mostly blended. Continue mixing, gradually increasing the speed, until the mixture is smooth. Add the Pastry Crunch and pulse to blend. Pour the smoothie into a glass and garnish with an Apple Chip (page 210), if desired.

Chocolate Coconut Island Breeze

The tropical flavors dominating this paradisiacal smoothie blend into a rich and sensual delight.

1 SERVING

⅔ to ¾ cup pineapple juice
1 cup partially frozen diced pineapple
½ cup partially frozen diced banana
2 tablespoons Chocolate Coconut Sauce (page 185)
½ to ¾ cup macadamia brittle or
    favorite vanilla ice cream

Place all the ingredients in a blender and mix by using the on/off pulse function until the ingredients are mostly blended. Continue mixing, gradually increasing the speed, until the mixture is smooth. Pour the smoothie into a glass and garnish with a Pineapple Chip (page 231), if desired.

Chocolate-Covered Halvah Smoothie

Halvah is a Middle Eastern sweet made of sesame seeds and honey and is found in most delicatessens or Asian or Middle Eastern food shops. Here, it contributes to a uniquely sweet smoothie.

1 SERVING

½ to ⅔ cup milk
2 tablespoons Chocolate Sauce (page 190)
1 cup partially frozen diced banana
⅓ cup (3 ounces) chocolate-covered or plain halvah, broken into small pieces
½ cup vanilla ice cream

Place all the ingredients in a blender and mix by using the on/off pulse function until the ingredients are mostly blended. Continue mixing, gradually increasing the speed, until the mixture is smooth. Pour the smoothie into a glass and garnish with a Chocolate-Dipped Frozen Baby Banana (page 217), if desired.

Chocolate Malt Smoothie

If you have a craving for something that is unashamedly rich, chocolate to the core, and unforgettably delectable, you must try this Chocolate Malt Smoothie.

1 SERVING

½ to ⅔ cup milk
2 tablespoons Chocolate Syrup (page 191)
1 cup partially frozen diced banana
⅓ cup malt powder
½ cup chocolate ice cream

Place all the ingredients in a blender and mix by using the on/off pulse function until the ingredients are mostly blended. Continue mixing, gradually increasing the speed, until the mixture is smooth. Pour the smoothie into a glass and garnish with a Chocolate Pirouette (page 213), if desired.

Coffee and Hazelnut Extraordinaire

There is something mysteriously delicious about a blend of coffee, banana, chocolate, and hazelnut praline. Whatever it is, this smoothie is not for the faint of heart.

1 SERVING

½ to ⅔ cup milk

2 tablespoons coffee extract, or to taste

3 to 4 tablespoons Chocolate Syrup (page 191)

1 cup partially frozen diced banana

2 to 3 tablespoons coarsely chopped
   Hazelnut Praline Crunch (page 199)

½ cup coffee ice cream

Place the milk, coffee extract, 3 tablespoons Chocolate Syrup, banana, Praline Crunch, and ice cream in a blender and mix by using the on/off pulse function until the ingredients are mostly blended. Continue mixing, gradually increasing the speed, until the mixture is smooth. If you like, spoon 1 tablespoon Chocolate Syrup in the bottom of a glass and add the smoothie. Garnish with a Chocolate-Dipped Frozen Baby Banana (page 217), if desired.

Coffee Lover's Temptation

You not only get a double dose of chocolate in this smoothie, but the banana adds a rich creamy flavor and the coffee extract gives it a buzz.

1 SERVING

½ to ⅔ cup milk
¼ cup coffee extract, or to taste
2 tablespoons Sugar's Hot Fudge Sauce (page 206)
1 cup partially frozen diced banana
½ cup chocolate malt ice cream

Place all the ingredients in a blender and mix by using the on/off pulse function until the ingredients are mostly blended. Continue mixing, gradually increasing the speed, until the mixture is smooth. Pour the smoothie into a glass and top with Chocolate Crunch (page 186), if desired.

Cookies and Cream

Who doesn't fret about not being able to eat just one Oreo cookie? Well, there are times in your life when you simply need to be reckless and carefree. When you're having one of those days, whip up this devilish combination of banana, Oreo cookies, and coffee ice cream—and don't forget to garnish it with a Chocolate-Covered Oreo Cookie.

1 SERVING

½ to ⅔ cup milk
1 cup partially frozen diced banana
½ cup coffee ice cream
6 Oreo or favorite chocolate sandwich cookies, crushed

Place the milk, banana, and ice cream in a blender and mix by using the on/off pulse function until the ingredients are mostly blended. Continue mixing, gradually increasing the speed, until the mixture is smooth. Add the cookies and pulse to blend. Pour the smoothie into a glass and garnish with a Chocolate-Covered Oreo Cookie (page 215), if desired.

German Chocolate Smoothie

Believe it or not, German chocolate cake is an American creation. In 1852, Sam German created a mild, dark baking chocolate bar for the Baker's Chocolate Co., and it was named in his honor: Baker's German's Sweet Chocolate. The first recipe for German chocolate cake appeared in a Dallas newspaper in 1957 and came from a Texas homemaker. Whoever thought this luscious bakery treat could morph into an equally delectable smoothie?

1 SERVING

½ to ⅔ cup milk

2 to 3 tablespoons German Chocolate Sauce (page 192)

1 cup partially frozen diced banana

2 tablespoons chopped pecans

½ cup Almond Joy or favorite coconut or
   vanilla ice cream

Place the milk, 2 tablespoons German Chocolate Sauce, the banana, pecans, and ice cream in a blender and mix by using the on/off pulse function until the ingredients are mostly blended. Continue mixing, gradually increasing the speed, until the mixture is smooth. If you like, spoon 1 tablespoon German Chocolate Sauce in the bottom of a glass and add the smoothie. Garnish with a Vanilla Pirouette (page 213), if desired.

Hazelnut, Banana, and Coffee Seduction

The essence of hazelnut syrup marries well with Milk Chocolate Sauce, banana, and coffee ice cream in this refreshing temptation. It's definitely a five-star smoothie.

1 SERVING

½ to ⅔ cup milk
2 tablespoons hazelnut syrup or coffee extract
2 tablespoons Milk Chocolate Sauce (page 197)
1 cup partially frozen diced banana
½ cup coffee ice cream

Place all the ingredients in a blender and mix by using the on/off pulse function until the ingredients are mostly blended. Continue mixing, gradually increasing the speed, until the mixture is smooth. Pour the smoothie into a glass and garnish with a Chocolate-Dipped Frozen Baby Banana (page 217), if desired.

Malted Milk Ball Smoothie

In 1949, malted milk balls candy was introduced under the name of Whoppers. When this candy is combined with banana, Milk Chocolate Sauce, and coffee ice cream, you get a whopper of a smoothie. Re-create a Saturday at the movies in your own home by serving this classic while enjoying your favorite DVD.

1 SERVING

½ to ⅔ cup milk
1 cup partially frozen diced banana
2 tablespoons Milk Chocolate Sauce (page 197)
½ cup coffee ice cream
½ cup malted milk balls, crushed

Place the milk, banana, Milk Chocolate Sauce, and ice cream in a blender and mix by using the on/off pulse function until the ingredients are mostly blended. Continue mixing, gradually increasing the speed, until the mixture is smooth. Add the malted milk balls and pulse to blend. Pour the smoothie into a glass and garnish with a Chocolate-Dipped Tortilla Triangle (page 221), if desired.

Mango and Macadamia Nut Enchantment

It almost makes you shudder when you think about the incredibly seductive ingredients that make up this smoothie. You might have to enjoy this one in private.

1 SERVING

⅔ to ¾ cup mango nectar

3 tablespoons Caramel Sauce (page 182)

1 ½ cups partially frozen diced mango

2 tablespoons coarsely chopped
    Macadamia Nut Praline Crunch (page 193)

¼ teaspoon ground cinnamon

⅛ teaspoon ground nutmeg

½ cup pralines and cream ice cream

Place all the ingredients in a blender and mix by using the on/off pulse function until the ingredients are mostly blended. Continue mixing, gradually increasing the speed, until the mixture is smooth. Pour the smoothie into a glass and garnish with a Cinnamon Pirouette (page 213), if desired.

Mint Oreo and Chocolate Decadence

Beware: This is not your ordinary cookie con-
coction in a glass. It's a delectable no-holds-
barred smoothie made with irresistible mint
Oreo cookies and seductive mint chip ice
cream. Drink with care.

1 SERVING

½ to ⅔ cup milk
2 tablespoons Chocolate Syrup (page 191)
1 cup partially frozen diced banana
½ cup mint chip ice cream
6 mint Oreo or favorite chocolate mint
    sandwich cookies, crushed

Place the milk, Chocolate Syrup, banana, and ice
cream in a blender and mix by using the on/off pulse
function until the ingredients are mostly blended.
Continue mixing, gradually increasing the speed,
until the mixture is smooth. Add the cookies and
pulse to blend. Pour the smoothie into a glass and
garnish with a Chocolate-Covered Oreo Cookie
(page 215), preferably a mint cookie, if desired.

Mochacchino Smoothie

Do you have a craving for chocolate or a spoon-ful of tempting ice cream? Are you looking for a little mischief in your life? Whip up a glassful of this sexy creation and let the fun begin.

1 SERVING

½ to ⅔ cup chilled espresso or strong coffee
1 cup partially frozen diced banana
2 tablespoons Chocolate Sauce (page 190)
½ cup Godiva Vanilla Caramel Pecan or
    favorite vanilla or coffee ice cream

Place all the ingredients in a blender and mix by using the on/off pulse function until the ingredients are mostly blended. Continue mixing, gradually increasing the speed, until the mixture is smooth. Pour the smoothie into a glass and garnish with a Chocolate Pirouette (page 213), if desired.

Orange, Caramel, and Praline Passion

This spellbinding smoothie is full of naturally sweet and seductive flavors. If you have some praline in your larder, add a few tablespoons to add crunch to this sweet creation.

1 SERVING

⅔ to ¾ cup orange juice
1 ½ cups partially frozen diced orange
2 to 3 tablespoons Caramel Sauce (page 182)
½ to ¾ cup pralines and cream ice cream

Place all the ingredients in a blender and mix by using the on/off pulse function until the ingredients are mostly blended. Continue mixing, gradually increasing the speed, until the mixture is smooth. Pour the smoothie into a glass and garnish with a Cinnamon Wonton Crisp (page 223), if desired.

Peach and Caramel Excitement

A rich caramel sauce and a hint of cinnamon partner well with peaches. Teaming these ingredients with macadamia brittle ice cream results in a richly flavored smoothie, the taste of which will linger long after the last sip.

1 SERVING

⅔ to ¾ cup peach nectar
3 tablespoons Caramel Sauce (page 182)
1 teaspoon honey, or to taste
1 ½ cups partially frozen diced peach
¼ teaspoon ground cinnamon
½ to ¾ cup macadamia brittle or
  favorite vanilla ice cream

Place all the ingredients in a blender and mix by using the on/off pulse function until the ingredients are mostly blended. Continue mixing, gradually increasing the speed, until the mixture is smooth. Pour the smoothie into a glass and garnish with a Cinnamon and Sugar Twist (page 219), if desired.

Peach and Praline Indulgence

Need a break from your diet? This seductive peach smoothie is quick and easy to prepare and satisfies your cravings instantly.

1 SERVING

⅔ to ¾ cup peach nectar

3 tablespoons Praline Sauce (page 203)

1 ½ cups partially frozen diced peach

½ cup Godiva Vanilla Caramel Pecan or
     favorite pralines and cream ice cream

Place all the ingredients in a blender and mix by using the on/off pulse function until the ingredients are mostly blended. Continue mixing, gradually increasing the speed, until the mixture is smooth. Pour the smoothie into a glass and garnish with a Vanilla Pirouette (page 213), if desired.

Pear, Banana, and Caramel Delirium

This pear, banana, and caramel smoothie is in a class by itself. Its haunting flavors will leave you in a state of sheer happiness.

1 SERVING

⅔ to ¾ cup milk
2 to 3 tablespoons Caramel Sauce (page 182)
1 cup partially frozen diced pear
½ cup partially frozen diced banana
½ cup Godiva Vanilla Caramel Pecan or
    favorite vanilla ice cream

Place all the ingredients in a blender and mix by using the on/off pulse function until the ingredients are mostly blended. Continue mixing, gradually increasing the speed, until the mixture is smooth. Pour the smoothie into a glass and garnish with a Pear Chip (page 229), if desired.

Pear Belle-Hélène Smoothie

Several different belle-Hélène recipes were introduced around 1865 by renowned Paris chefs, with the title referring to an operetta by Offenbach. One of the most outstanding of these recipes was for pears Belle-Hélène, a cold pear and chocolate dessert that you can now enjoy as a unique smoothie.

1 SERVING

3 ripe Bosc pears
1 quart cold water
¾ cup sugar
¼ cup fresh lemon juice
1 to 2 teaspoons finely grated lemon zest
1 tablespoon pure vanilla extract
⅔ cup milk or pear nectar
2 tablespoons Sugar's Hot Fudge Sauce (page 206)
½ cup vanilla bean ice cream

Using a piece of parchment paper, make a lid to cover the pears by cutting out a round disk that is slightly smaller than the diameter of the pan you will be using to poach the pears. Line a baking sheet with freezer paper. Set aside.

RECIPE CONTINUES

Peel the pears and leave the stems intact. Using a melon baller or an apple corer, remove the core from the bottom of the pears (be careful not to break or split the sides of the pear).

Combine the water, sugar, lemon juice, lemon zest, and vanilla in a nonreactive heavy medium saucepan and place over medium-high heat. Place the pears on their sides in the poaching liquid and bring to a boil. Reduce the heat to a simmer, cover the pears with the parchment lid, and cook for about 40 to 50 minutes, or until the pears can be pierced easily with a wooden skewer or toothpick, turning the pears occasionally. Remove the pears from the liquid and place them on the prepared baking sheet to cool. Once the pears are cool, remove and discard the stems and cut each pear into quarters. Freeze the pears for 1 hour or more.

When you are ready to make the smoothie, place the milk, pears, Hot Fudge Sauce, and ice cream in a blender and mix by using the on/off pulse function until the ingredients are mostly blended. Continue mixing, gradually increasing the speed, until the mixture is smooth. Pour the smoothie into a glass and garnish with a Pear Chip (page 229), if desired.

Pineapple and Caramel Seduction

You won't believe your good fortune after one taste of this simple, yet pleasing combination of Caramel Sauce, pineapple, and a lusciously rich rum raisin ice cream.

1 SERVING

⅔ to ¾ cup orange juice
2 to 3 tablespoons Caramel Sauce (page 182)
1 ½ cups partially frozen diced pineapple
½ cup rum raisin or favorite vanilla ice cream

Place all the ingredients in a blender and mix by using the on/off pulse function until the ingredients are mostly blended. Continue mixing, gradually increasing the speed, until the mixture is smooth. Pour the smoothie into a glass and garnish with a Cinnamon and Sugar Twist (page 219), if desired.

Pineapple and Raspberry Crunch Smoothie

This smoothie is definitely for the rich and famished. Pineapple and raspberries are paired with mouthwatering white chocolate and raspberry ice cream and a luscious chocolate, nut, and raisin crunch.

1 SERVING

⅔ to ¾ cup milk

1 cup partially frozen diced pineapple

½ cup partially frozen raspberries

¼ cup Chocolate, Nut, and Raisin Crunch (page 188)

½ cup Godiva White Chocolate Raspberry or
    favorite vanilla or white chocolate ice cream

Place all the ingredients in a blender and mix by using the on/off pulse function until the ingredients are mostly blended. Continue mixing, gradually increasing the speed, until the mixture is smooth. Pour the smoothie into a glass and garnish with a Vanilla Pirouette (page 213), if desired.

Pineapple, Banana, and Praline Temptation

The next time you have a craving for something incredibly sweet and naughty, whip up a blender full of this New Orleans–inspired smoothie.

1 SERVING

⅔ to ¾ cup pineapple juice
2 to 3 tablespoons Praline Sauce (page 203)
1 cup partially frozen diced banana
½ cup partially frozen diced pineapple
2 tablespoons coarsely chopped
    Pecan Praline Crunch (page 199) (optional)
½ cup pralines and cream ice cream

Place all the ingredients in a blender and mix by using the on/off pulse function until the ingredients are mostly blended. Continue mixing, gradually increasing the speed, until the mixture is smooth. Pour the smoothie into a glass and garnish with a Crisp Banana Wafer (page 225), if desired.

Pineapple, Caramel, and Macadamia Nut Orgy

This smoothie defines seduction. How can anyone resist such incredible ingredients wrapped
up in a glassful of heaven?

1 SERVING

⅔ to ¾ cup pineapple juice
2 tablespoons Caramel Sauce (page 182)
1 ½ cups partially frozen diced pineapple
2 tablespoons coarsely chopped Macadamia Nut
    Praline Crunch (page 193)
½ cup macadamia brittle or
    favorite pralines and cream ice cream

Place all the ingredients in a blender and mix by
using the on/off pulse function until the ingredients
are mostly blended. Continue mixing, gradually
increasing the speed, until the mixture is smooth.
Pour the smoothie into a glass and garnish with a
Vanilla Pirouette (page 213), if desired.

Pineapple Delight

This sensuous, naughty smoothie is made with pineapple, a rich caramel sauce, and macadamia brittle ice cream. To make this delectable treat even more decadent, dip the rim of a cocktail glass in melted white chocolate, then dip or sprinkle with multicolored nonpareils or party sugar, and use for serving.

1 SERVING

⅔ to ¾ cup pineapple juice
1 teaspoon honey, or to taste (optional)
1 ½ cups partially frozen diced pineapple
3 tablespoons Caramel Sauce (page 182)
¾ cup macadamia brittle or favorite vanilla ice cream

Place all the ingredients in a blender and mix by using the on/off pulse function until the ingredients are mostly blended. Continue mixing, gradually increasing the speed, until the mixture is smooth. Pour the smoothie into a glass and garnish with a Cinnamon-Dipped Tortilla Triangle (page 221), if desired.

Pralines Pecan Pie Smoothie

This classic pecan pie smoothie makes the perfect dessert to serve after a meal or anytime you're in the mood for some sumptuous Southern living.

1 SERVING

½ to ⅔ cup milk

2 tablespoons Praline Sauce (page 203)

1 cup partially frozen diced banana

2 tablespoons coarsely chopped
    Pecan Praline Crunch (page 199) (optional)

½ cup butter pecan or
    favorite pralines and cream ice cream

Place all the ingredients in a blender and mix by using the on/off pulse function until the ingredients are mostly blended. Continue mixing, gradually increasing the speed, until the mixture is smooth. Pour the smoothie into a glass and garnish with a Cinnamon and Sugar Twist (page 219), if desired.

South-of-the-Border Sundae

The simple banana smoothie can be elevated to new heights when made with sumptuous South-of-the-Border Chocolate Sauce. However, it would taste almost as divine made with your favorite chocolate syrup.

1 SERVING

½ to ⅔ cup milk

1 cup partially frozen diced banana

2 tablespoons South-of-the-Border Chocolate Sauce (page 205) or favorite chocolate syrup

½ cup coffee or favorite caramel or vanilla ice cream

Place all the ingredients in a blender and mix by using the on/off pulse function until the ingredients are mostly blended. Continue mixing, gradually increasing the speed, until the mixture is smooth. Pour the smoothie into a glass and garnish with a Cinnamon Wonton Crisp (page 223), if desired.

Too Minty for Words

Chocolate-covered mints and mint chip ice cream make this banana smoothie utterly fantastic!

1 SERVING

½ to ⅔ cup milk
4 ounces chocolate-covered mints, diced
1 cup partially frozen diced banana
½ cup mint chip ice cream

Place all the ingredients in a blender and mix by using the on/off pulse function until the ingredients are mostly blended. Continue mixing, gradually increasing the speed, until the mixture is smooth. Pour the smoothie into a glass and garnish with a Chocolate-Covered Oreo Cookie (page 215), preferably a mint cookie, if desired.

Tropical Fruit and Coconut Pleasure

The tropical fruit flavors are accentuated by the luscious Caramel Sauce in this mouthwatering smoothie. For some added excitement, serve it in a hollowed-out coconut shell and garnish with an orchid.

1 SERVING

⅔ to ¾ cup mango nectar
½ cup partially frozen diced pineapple
½ cup partially frozen diced mango
½ cup partially frozen diced banana
3 tablespoons Caramel Sauce (page 182)
½ cup coconut gelato or favorite coconut or
    vanilla ice cream

Place all the ingredients in a blender and mix by using the on/off pulse function until the ingredients are mostly blended. Continue mixing, gradually increasing the speed, until the mixture is smooth. Pour the smoothie into a glass and garnish with a Cinnamon-Dipped Tortilla Triangle (page 221), if desired.

Tropical Sundae

This richly flavored smoothie is the perfect creation to serve at your next luau or anytime you have a craving for something tropical and out of the ordinary.

1 SERVING

⅔ to ¾ cup pineapple juice
1 teaspoon honey, or to taste (optional)
¾ cup partially frozen diced pineapple
¾ cup partially frozen diced banana
2 to 3 tablespoons Caramel Sauce (page 182)
½ cup coconut gelato or favorite coconut or
    vanilla ice cream

Place all the ingredients in a blender and mix by using the on/off pulse function until the ingredients are mostly blended. Continue mixing, gradually increasing the speed, until the mixture is smooth. Pour the smoothie into a glass and garnish with a Vanilla Pirouette (page 213), if desired.

Turtle Smoothie

This smoothie is for the turtleholic. Two irresistible sauces, caramel and hot fudge, along with banana and toffee ice cream are melded together into a treat to die for. It will leave you gasping for air—or, should I say, grasping for more.

1 SERVING

½ to ⅔ cup milk

2 tablespoons Sugar's Hot Fudge Sauce (page 206)

2 tablespoons Caramel Sauce (page 182)

1 cup partially frozen diced banana

½ cup Dreamery Caramel Toffee Bar Heaven or favorite toffee ice cream

Place all the ingredients in a blender and mix by using the on/off pulse function until the ingredients are mostly blended. Continue mixing, gradually increasing the speed, until the mixture is smooth. Pour the smoothie into a glass and garnish with a Turtle on a Skewer (page 234), if desired.

5

Happy-Hour Smoothies

Cocktails That Satisfy Your Sweet Tooth

---

*I have taken more out of alcohol
than alcohol has taken out of me.*

—Winston Churchill
(1874–1965)

WHAT MAKES SMOOTHIES ALL THE RAGE IS THAT
these mellow concoctions are made from a simple
union of fruit and fruit juice, resulting in a delightful combination that is easy to prepare and tastes
great. However, the addition of liqueur or spirits to
many of your favorite smoothie ingredients can
result in an uptown temptation that reaches a
dimension of elegance and seduction never before
dreamed of. And the union of spirits and smoothies
doesn't end here. With the addition of rich, creamy
ice cream and garnished with a Chocolate Pirouette
or a Cinnamon and Sugar Twist, these showstop-
ping creations can even grace an elegant dessert
plate as the grand finale of a candlelight dinner.

As you glance at the spiked delights found in this chapter, you will see some that are smoothie versions of familiar cocktails, such as the Piña Colada Smoothie. Other happy-hour smoothies are intended to be enjoyed as a dessert. Try enhancing your after-meal pleasure with a serving of Frozen Cappuccino, a mouthwatering blend of Irish cream liqueur, Kahlúa, hazelnut liqueur, banana, and vanilla ice cream. Prepare yourself for the ultimate experience when you indulge in a glassful of a Death by Chocolate Smoothie cocktail, featuring the wonderful essence of Irish cream liqueur, brown crème de cacao, and vodka. Make sure to double the recipe, so you can share this sensual experience with someone special.

In the new millennium, I can't think of a more appropriate celebration than smoothies newly transformed into seductively delicious treats that will leave you begging for more. So get out your swizzle sticks and fancy crystal, and experience the pleasure of indulging in any one of these sensuous alcoholic delights.

Arctic Joy Smoothie

Cool down with a refreshing glassful of this sub-lime smoothie highlighted with mint liqueur and ice cream. It's rich enough to be served as a dessert or as an after-dinner treat.

1 SERVING

¼ cup milk
2 tablespoons white crème de menthe
2 tablespoons white crème de cacao
1 tablespoon Chocolate Syrup (page 191)
1 cup partially frozen diced banana
½ cup mint chip ice cream

Place all the ingredients in a blender and mix by using the on/off pulse function until the ingredients are mostly blended. Continue mixing, gradually increasing the speed, until the mixture is smooth. Pour the smoothie into a glass and garnish with a Chocolate-Covered Oreo Cookie (page 215), prefer-ably a mint cookie, if desired.

Baileys Banana Colada

This smoothie is so easy to prepare, yet it's fantastically rich and flavorful.

1 SERVING

2 tablespoons crème de banana or
     other banana liqueur
2 tablespoons Baileys Original Irish Cream or
     other Irish cream liqueur
1 cup partially frozen diced banana
½ cup coconut gelato or favorite coconut or
     vanilla ice cream

Place all the ingredients in a blender and mix by using the on/off pulse function until the ingredients are mostly blended. Continue mixing, gradually increasing the speed, until the mixture is smooth. Pour the smoothie into a glass and garnish with a Crisp Banana Wafer (page 225), if desired.

Baileys Cappuccino

If you're looking for an unusual dessert or just crave something sweet in the afternoon, try this temptingly delicious coffee-and-chocolate-flavored smoothie with a little kick from the Emerald Isle.

1 SERVING

⅓ cup milk

3 tablespoons Baileys Original Irish Cream or
    other Irish cream liqueur

1 cup partially frozen diced banana

1 .58-oz. package Maxwell House
    French Vanilla Iced Cappuccino mix

2 tablespoons Chocolate Syrup (page 191)

½ cup vanilla or coffee ice cream

Place all the ingredients in a blender and mix by using the on/off pulse function until the ingredients are mostly blended. Continue mixing, gradually increasing the speed, until the mixture is smooth. Pour the smoothie into a glass and garnish with a Chocolate Pirouette (page 213), if desired.

Baileys Chocolate Shake

This Baileys Chocolate Shake promises to satisfy any cravings you may have for something that tastes rich, sweet, and irresistibly delicious.

1 SERVING

¼ cup Baileys Original Irish Cream or
    other Irish cream liqeur
¼ cup milk
Chocolate Syrup (page 191)
1 cup partially frozen diced banana
½ cup vanilla ice cream

Place the Irish cream, milk, 2 tablespoons Chocolate Syrup, the banana, and ice cream in a blender and mix by using the on/off pulse function until the ingredients are mostly blended. Continue mixing, gradually increasing the speed, until the mixture is smooth. If you like, spoon 1 to 2 teaspoons Chocolate Syrup in the bottom of a glass and add the smoothie. Garnish with a Chocolate-Covered Oreo Cookie (page 215), if desired.

Banana and Frangelico Espresso

Frangelico is a proprietary liqueur known for its wonderful hazelnut flavor. When added to coffee and other smoothie ingredients, the elegantly balanced combination that results is a temptingly delicious cupful of happiness.

1 SERVING

¼ cup Frangelico liqueur or other hazelnut liqueur
2 tablespoons chilled espresso or strong coffee
1 cup partially frozen diced banana
½ cup coffee ice cream

Place all the ingredients in a blender and mix by using the on/off pulse function until the ingredients are mostly blended. Continue mixing, gradually increasing the speed, until the mixture is smooth. Pour the smoothie into a glass and garnish with a Cinnamon-Dipped Tortilla Triangle (page 221), if desired.

Banana, Caramel, and Port Indulgence

An occasional indulgence is good for the soul, especially when it's a pleasurable glassful, such as this remarkable smoothie made with port, caramel, and a too, too rich ice cream.

1 SERVING

⅓ cup milk

2 tablespoons port

2 to 3 tablespoons Caramel Sauce (page 182)

1 cup partially frozen diced banana

½ cup Godiva Vanilla Caramel Pecan or favorite
   vanilla ice cream

Place all the ingredients in a blender and mix by using the on/off pulse function until the ingredients are mostly blended. Continue mixing, gradually increasing the speed, until the mixture is smooth. Pour the smoothie into a glass and garnish with a Cinnamon and Sugar Twist (page 219), if desired.

Banana Rum Splendor

This pleasingly sweet blend of fruit flavors carries a Caribbean kick.

1 SERVING

2 large bananas, cut into chunks
2 tablespoons firmly packed dark brown sugar
¼ teaspoon ground cinnamon
2 teaspoons unsalted butter, cut into small pieces
⅓ cup orange juice
2 tablespoons dark rum
½ cup Godiva Vanilla Caramel Pecan or
   favorite vanilla ice cream

Preheat the oven to 350°F. Place a strainer over a medium bowl. Line a baking sheet with freezer paper. Set aside.

Place the bananas in an ovenproof dish and sprinkle with the brown sugar, cinnamon, and butter pieces. Pour the orange juice over all. Bake for 15 minutes. Remove the dish from the oven and place it on a cooling rack. When the banana mixture is cool, transfer it to the strainer over the bowl (reserve the liquid). Place the bananas on the prepared baking sheet and freeze for 1 hour or more. Cover the bowl containing the liquid and refrigerate.

When you are ready to make the smoothie, place the reserved liquid, rum, bananas, and ice cream in a blender and mix by using the on/off pulse function until the ingredients are mostly blended. Continue mixing, gradually increasing the speed, until the mixture is smooth. Pour the smoothie into a glass and garnish with a Cinnamon Pirouette (page 213), if desired.

Bananas Foster

This fabulous dessert was created at New Orleans's Brennan's restaurant in the 1950s. It was named for Richard Foster, who was a regular Brennan's patron. One taste of the decadently rich smoothie version of this classic and you'll be happy Mr. Foster was such a faithful customer.

1 SERVING

2 tablespoons (¼ stick) unsalted butter
¼ cup firmly packed dark brown sugar
¼ teaspoon ground cinnamon
⅛ teaspoon ground nutmeg
2 bananas, cut into chunks
¼ cup dark rum
2 tablespoons crème de banana or
   other banana liqueur
⅓ cup milk
½ cup vanilla ice cream

Line a shallow bowl with nonstick aluminum foil. Set aside.

Melt the butter in a medium sauté pan over medium heat. Swirl the pan to coat evenly. Add the brown sugar, cinnamon, and nutmeg and stir to make a paste. Cook for 2 minutes, stirring occasionally. Increase the heat to medium-high and add the bananas, rum, and banana liqueur and cook for 3 minutes, or until the sauce is hot, shaking the pan back and forth occasionally. Tip the pan slightly and use a long matchstick to ignite the sauce (or simply allow the mixture to boil for a minute or two). When the flames subside, remove the pan from the heat and place it on a cooling rack. When the banana mixture is cool, transfer it to the prepared bowl and freeze for 1 hour or more.

When you are ready to make the smoothie, place the milk, banana mixture, and ice cream in a blender and mix by using the on/off pulse function until the ingredients are mostly blended. Continue mixing, gradually increasing the speed, until the mixture is smooth. Pour the smoothie into a glass and garnish with a Cinnamon Wonton Crisp (page 223), if desired.

Blizzard Smoothie

Liquor rules in this enticing smoothie! Serve this seductive delight the next time there is a full moon.

1 SERVING

1 tablespoon brandy
1 tablespoon Irish cream liqueur
1 tablespoon Kahlúa or other coffee liqueur
1 tablespoon light rum
1 cup partially frozen diced banana
½ cup vanilla ice cream

Place all the ingredients in a blender and mix by using the on/off pulse function until the ingredients are mostly blended. Continue mixing, gradually increasing the speed, until the mixture is smooth. Pour the smoothie into a glass and garnish with a Chocolate-Dipped Frozen Baby Banana (page 217), if desired.

Cappuccino Royale

Tie one on after a quiet dinner by serving this seductive rum and brandy coffee creation.

1 SERVING

3 tablespoons chilled espresso or strong coffee
1 tablespoon light rum
1 tablespoon brandy
1 tablespoon brown crème de cacao
2 to 3 teaspoons honey, or to taste
1 cup partially frozen diced banana
½ cup vanilla ice cream

Place all the ingredients in a blender and mix by using the on/off pulse function until the ingredients are mostly blended. Continue mixing, gradually increasing the speed, until the mixture is smooth. Pour the smoothie into a glass and garnish with a Vanilla Pirouette (page 213), if desired.

Chilly Leprechaun Smoothie

Beware! This delectable smoothie is not for the faint of heart. Oozing with flavors of coffee and spirits, it's the perfect elixir to serve on St. Pat's Day.

1 SERVING

¼ cup chilled espresso or strong coffee
2 tablespoons Irish whiskey
1 tablespoon Irish cream liqueur
1 tablespoon Kahlúa or other coffee liqueur
1 cup partially frozen diced banana
½ cup vanilla ice cream

Place all the ingredients in a blender and mix by using the on/off pulse function until the ingredients are mostly blended. Continue mixing, gradually increasing the speed, until the mixture is smooth. Pour the smoothie into a glass and garnish with a Crisp Banana Wafer (page 225), if desired.

Chocolate Almond Cream

If amaretto is one of your favorite liqueurs, then you are certain to fall in love with this sensational smoothie.

1 SERVING

2 tablespoons amaretto
2 tablespoons brown crème de cacao
1 cup partially frozen diced banana
½ to ¾ cup vanilla ice cream

Place all the ingredients in a blender and mix by using the on/off pulse function until the ingredients are mostly blended. Continue mixing, gradually increasing the speed, until the mixture is smooth. Pour the smoothie into a glass and garnish with a Cinnamon and Sugar Twist (page 219) or top with chocolate shavings, if desired.

Clementine, Raspberry, and Grand Marnier Madness

You'll be deliriously happy after one taste of this invitingly decadent smoothie. One can only wonder how such simple ingredients can produce such pleasure.

1 SERVING

⅓ cup milk

2 tablespoons Grand Marnier or other orange liqueur

1 teaspoon honey, or to taste

1 cup partially frozen diced clementines or seedless tangerines

½ cup partially frozen raspberries

½ cup Godiva White Chocolate Raspberry or favorite vanilla or white chocolate ice cream

Place all the ingredients in a blender and mix by using the on/off pulse function until the ingredients are mostly blended. Continue mixing, gradually increasing the speed, until the mixture is smooth. Pour the smoothie into a glass and garnish with Berries on a Skewer (page 212), if desired.

Creamsicle

Like its cousin on a stick, this grown-up version
never fails to delight.

1 SERVING

3 tablespoons Grand Marnier or other orange liqueur
3 tablespoons Galliano
1 ½ cups partially frozen diced orange
½ cup vanilla ice cream

Place all the ingredients in a blender and mix by
using the on/off pulse function until the ingredients
are mostly blended. Continue mixing, gradually
increasing the speed, until the mixture is smooth.
Pour the smoothie into a glass and garnish with a
Cinnamon Wonton Crisp (page 223), if desired.

Death by Chocolate Smoothie

For the ultimate chocolate experience, dip the rim of a cocktail glass in melted chocolate, then place it in the freezer to allow the chocolate to set, or moisten the rim with crème de cacao and dip in powdered chocolate (see Note). Serve this extravagant smoothie in the decked-out glass and wait for the raves!

1 SERVING

2 tablespoons Irish cream liqueur
1 tablespoon brown crème de cacao
1 tablespoon vodka
1 cup partially frozen diced banana
½ cup chocolate gelato or
    favorite chocolate ice cream

Place all the ingredients in a blender and mix by using the on/off pulse function until the ingredients are mostly blended. Continue mixing, gradually increasing the speed, until the mixture is smooth. Pour the smoothie into a glass and garnish with a Chocolate Pirouette (page 213), if desired.

NOTE: Les Confitures à l'Ancienne Powdered Chocolate is a drinking hot cocoa with raw cane sugar that is imported from France. It is available on the Web at www.cybercucina.com. When you get to the site, look for "Quick Clicks" on the left-hand side of the page, then scroll down to "Candies/Chocolate." Choose these words and you'll find a selection of sweets, including this special powdered chocolate.

Frozen Cappuccino

Cappuccino is named after the brown robes worn by Capuchin monks. This Frozen Cappuccino smoothie can be served as a sumptuous dessert after an elegant dinner or as a naughty indulgence in the afternoon.

1 SERVING

1 ½ tablespoons Irish cream liqueur
1 ½ tablespoons Kahlúa or other coffee liqueur
1 ½ tablespoons hazelnut liqueur
1 cup partially frozen diced banana
½ cup vanilla ice cream

Place all the ingredients in a blender and mix by using the on/off pulse function until the ingredients are mostly blended. Continue mixing, gradually increasing the speed, until the mixture is smooth. Pour the smoothie into a glass and garnish with a Chocolate-Dipped Frozen Baby Banana (page 217) or a dollop of whipped cream sprinkled with powdered chocolate, if desired.

Godiva Espresso

Let your hair down and indulge in this extravagant coffee pleasure. For an added touch, serve this delectable treat in a chocolate-rimmed cocktail glass (see Death by Chocolate Smoothie, page 148).

1 SERVING

¼ cup chilled espresso or strong coffee
3 tablespoons Godiva liqueur or
    other chocolate liqueur
1 cup partially frozen diced banana
¾ cup coffee ice cream

Place all the ingredients in a blender and mix by using the on/off pulse function until the ingredients are mostly blended. Continue mixing, gradually increasing the speed, until the mixture is smooth. Pour the smoothie into a glass and garnish with a Chocolate-Dipped Tortilla Triangle (page 221), if desired.

Goom Bay Smash

Serve this luscious tropical smoothie as a dessert or after-dinner refreshment when you are having friends over for a casual barbecue dinner.

1 SERVING

2 tablespoons dark or spiced rum

2 tablespoons coconut rum

1 tablespoon crème de banana or
    other banana liqueur

1 cup partially frozen diced pineapple

½ cup partially frozen diced orange

½ cup vanilla or favorite coconut ice cream

Place all the ingredients in a blender and mix by using the on/off pulse function until the ingredients are mostly blended. Continue mixing, gradually increasing the speed, until the mixture is smooth. Pour the smoothie into a glass and garnish with a Pineapple Chip (page 231), if desired.

Grasshopper Smoothie

The sweet, minty flavor of this smoothie makes it the perfect fare to serve as dessert or an after-dinner drink.

1 SERVING

2 tablespoons green crème de menthe
2 tablespoons white crème de cacao
1 cup partially frozen diced banana
¾ cup vanilla ice cream

Place all the ingredients in a blender and mix by using the on/off pulse function until the ingredients are mostly blended. Continue mixing, gradually increasing the speed, until the mixture is smooth. Pour the smoothie into a glass and garnish with a Chocolate-Covered Oreo Cookie (page 215), preferably a mint cookie, if desired.

Heather's Dream Smoothie

Sambuca is an Italian liqueur that gets its unique flavor from the infusion of witch elder bush and licorice. It is tradition to serve it with three or five coffee beans (the odd number is for good luck), so I encourage you to add them to this very special smoothie.

1 SERVING

3 tablespoons Sambuca

3 to 5 tablespoons peach nectar

1 ½ cups partially frozen diced peach

½ cup vanilla ice cream

3 coffee beans (optional)

Place the Sambuca, peach nectar, peach, and ice cream in a blender and mix by using the on/off pulse function until the ingredients are mostly blended. Continue mixing, gradually increasing the speed, until the mixture is smooth. Place the coffee beans, if using, in the bottom of a glass and add the smoothie. Garnish with a Vanilla Pirouette (page 213), if desired.

Irish Coffee Smoothie

As the Irish actor and musician Alex Levine once said, "Only Irish coffee provides in a single glass all four essential food groups: alcohol, caffeine, sugar, and fat." This creamy-rich smoothie version of the java classic keeps the tradition alive.

1 SERVING

2 tablespoons Irish whiskey
2 tablespoons Baileys Original Irish Cream or
    other Irish cream liqueur
1 cup partially frozen diced banana
½ to ¾ cup coffee ice cream

Place all the ingredients in a blender and mix by using the on/off pulse function until the ingredients are mostly blended. Continue mixing, gradually increasing the speed, until the mixture is smooth. Pour the smoothie into a glass and garnish with a Cinnamon-Dipped Tortilla Triangle (page 221), if desired.

Irish Dream

You'll find this smoothie to be so delicious, you'll be dreaming about it all night.

1 SERVING

2 tablespoons hazelnut liqueur
2 tablespoons Irish cream liqueur
1 tablespoon brown crème de cacao
1 cup partially frozen diced banana
½ cup vanilla ice cream

Place all the ingredients in a blender and mix by using the on/off pulse function until the ingredients are mostly blended. Continue mixing, gradually increasing the speed, until the mixture is smooth. Pour the smoothie into a glass and garnish with a dollop of whipped cream topped with chocolate sprinkles, if desired.

Italian Coffee

The only word that can describe this exquisite coffee, amaretto, and banana smoothie is *amore.*

1 SERVING

¼ cup chilled espresso or strong coffee
2 tablespoons amaretto
1 cup partially frozen diced banana
½ cup coffee ice cream

Place all the ingredients in a blender and mix by using the on/off pulse function until the ingredients are mostly blended. Continue mixing, gradually increasing the speed, until the mixture is smooth. Pour the smoothie into a glass and garnish with a Vanilla Pirouette (page 213), if desired.

Jamaican Coffee

It's hard to believe that anything so easy to prepare can taste so irresistibly delicious.

1 SERVING

2 tablespoons Kahlúa or other coffee liqueur
2 tablespoons light rum
1 cup partially frozen diced banana
½ cup coffee ice cream

Place all the ingredients in a blender and mix by
using the on/off pulse function until the ingredients
are mostly blended. Continue mixing, gradually
increasing the speed, until the mixture is smooth.
Pour the smoothie into a glass and garnish with a
Crisp Banana Wafer (page 225), if desired.

Kona Nut

This is another seductive creation that takes only minutes to prepare but should be sipped slowly so you can savor each individual ingredient.

1 SERVING

2 tablespoons Kahlúa or other coffee liqueur
2 tablespoons hazelnut liqueur
1 cup partially frozen diced banana
½ cup vanilla or favorite coffee ice cream

Place all the ingredients in a blender and mix by using the on/off pulse function until the ingredients are mostly blended. Continue mixing, gradually increasing the speed, until the mixture is smooth. Pour the smoothie into a glass and garnish with a Chocolate-Dipped Frozen Baby Banana (page 215), if desired.

Lesbos Island Snow Smoothie

Who could imagine that two of the most traditional ingredients used to make an everyday
smoothie could be so magically enhanced with
liqueurs and sweetened with luscious ice
cream?

1 SERVING

3 tablespoons strawberry liqueur
2 tablespoons crème de banana or
    other banana liqueur
½ cup partially frozen diced strawberries
½ cup partially frozen diced banana
½ cup vanilla ice cream

Place all the ingredients in a blender and mix by
using the on/off pulse function until the ingredients
are mostly blended. Continue mixing, gradually
increasing the speed, until the mixture is smooth.
Pour the smoothie into a glass and garnish with a
Strawberry Fan (page 233), if desired.

Midnight Mozart

If you've been looking for a seductive smoothie to serve someone special, this is it. Pour it into a wide-brimmed cocktail glass that has been dipped in chocolate (see Death by Chocolate Smoothie, page 00), add two straws, and share this pleasure together.

1 SERVING

3 tablespoons Mozart liqueur or
   other chocolate liqueur
3 tablespoons Kahlúa or other coffee liqueur
1 cup partially frozen diced banana
½ cup coffee ice cream

Place all the ingredients in a blender and mix by using the on/off pulse function until the ingredients are mostly blended. Continue mixing, gradually increasing the speed, until the mixture is smooth. Pour the smoothie into a glass and garnish with a Chocolate Pirouette (page 213), if desired.

Mocha Banana

Anything made with Kahlúa has to taste good, and this smoothie is no exception.

1 SERVING

¼ cup Kahlúa or other coffee liqueur
1 teaspoon honey, or to taste (optional)
1 cup partially frozen diced banana
1 cup coffee ice cream

Place all the ingredients in a blender and mix by using the on/off pulse function until the ingredients are mostly blended. Continue mixing, gradually increasing the speed, until the mixture is smooth. Pour the smoothie into a glass and garnish with a Chocolate-Dipped Tortilla Triangle (page 221), if desired.

Nutcracker

Talk about an opulent smoothie made with irresistible ingredients—this spirited combination will get your attention.

1 SERVING

2 tablespoons vodka
1 tablespoon Frangelico or other hazelnut liqueur
1 tablespoon amaretto
1 tablespoon Baileys Original Irish Cream or
    other Irish cream liqueur
1 cup partially frozen diced banana
½ cup vanilla ice cream

Place all the ingredients in a blender and mix by using the on/off pulse function until the ingredients are mostly blended. Continue mixing, gradually increasing the speed, until the mixture is smooth. Pour the smoothie into a glass and garnish with a Crisp Banana Wafer (page 225), if desired.

Oatmeal Cookie Smoothie

You can't help but be seduced by the complexity of flavors found in this tempting smoothie. For an added touch, serve with a plateful of your favorite oatmeal cookies.

1 SERVING

2 tablespoons cinnamon schnapps
1 tablespoon Irish cream liqueur
1 teaspoon Frangelico or other hazelnut liqueur
1 teaspoon Kahlúa or other coffee liqueur
1 cup partially frozen diced banana
½ to ¾ cup vanilla ice cream

Place all the ingredients in a blender and mix by using the on/off pulse function until the ingredients are mostly blended. Continue mixing, gradually increasing the speed, until the mixture is smooth. Pour the smoothie into a glass and garnish with a Cinnamon Pirouette (page 213), if desired.

Peanut Butter Cup Smoothie

There aren't enough superlatives to describe how sensational this smoothie is. How can you go wrong with such tantalizing ingredients?

1 SERVING

¼ cup Malibu coconut rum or other coconut rum
2 tablespoons Chocolate Syrup (page 191)
1 tablespoon vodka
1 cup partially frozen diced banana
1 tablespoon creamy peanut butter
½ cup vanilla ice cream

Place all the ingredients in a blender and mix by using the on/off pulse function until the ingredients are mostly blended. Continue mixing, gradually increasing the speed, until the mixture is smooth. Pour the smoothie into a glass and garnish with a Peanut Butter–Chocolate Drop (page 227), if desired.

Peppermint Penguin Smoothie

Imagine how refreshing this mint smoothie would taste after a savory barbecue meal during the hot and steamy days of summer.

1 SERVING

3 tablespoons chocolate mint liqueur
2 tablespoons green crème de menthe
1 cup partially frozen diced banana
½ cup mint chip or favorite vanilla ice cream
3 Oreo or favorite chocolate sandwich cookies, crushed

Place the chocolate mint liqueur, crème de menthe, banana, and ice cream in a blender and mix by using the on/off pulse function until the ingredients are mostly blended. Continue mixing, gradually increasing the speed, until the mixture is smooth. Add the cookies and pulse to blend. Pour the smoothie into a glass and garnish with a Chocolate-Covered Oreo Cookie (page 215), preferably a mint cookie, if desired.

Pie à la Mode

Licor 43 is a Spanish liqueur with a vanilla flavor. The formula for Licor 43 contains more than forty-three basic elements, mainly fruits and herbs, and has been passed down from generation to generation. Don't despair if you don't have this special liqueur, because vanilla vodka works almost as well.

1 SERVING

1 tablespoon Licor 43 or vanilla vodka
1 tablespoon vodka
1 tablespoon apple schnapps
1 tablespoon maple syrup, or to taste
1 ½ cups partially frozen diced apple
½ cup apple pie or favorite vanilla ice cream

Place all the ingredients in a blender and mix by using the on/off pulse function until the ingredients are mostly blended. Continue mixing, gradually increasing the speed, until the mixture is smooth. Pour the smoothie into a glass and garnish with a Cinnamon and Sugar Twist (page 219), if desired.

Piña Colada Smoothie

This version of Piña Colada Smoothie is from my *Tipsy Smoothies* cookbook. It is wonderful as is, but if you want to kick it up a notch, transform it into a bubble cocktail. If you don't already know about bubble cocktails, this craze originated in Taiwan about fifteen years ago. The unique ingredient that provides the bubbles is tapioca pearls, about the size of marbles and with a consistency like gummy candy (see Note). A special jumbo-sized straw, about one centimeter in diameter, is used to sip these large pearls and, of course, this delectable smoothie.

1 SERVING

3 tablespoons gold rum
1 tablespoon dark rum
1 ½ cups partially frozen diced pineapple
¾ cup coconut gelato or favorite coconut or
    vanilla ice cream
¼ to ½ cup cooked tapioca pearls (optional)

Place the rums, pineapple, and gelato in a blender and mix by using the on/off pulse function until the ingredients are mostly blended. Continue mixing, gradually increasing the speed, until the mixture is smooth. Place some tapioca pearls, if using, in the bottom of a glass and add the smoothie. Garnish with a Pineapple Chip (page 231) and serve with a jumbo-sized straw, if desired.

NOTE: To buy tapioca pearls and jumbo-sized straws, enter TenRen.com on the Web (or call toll-free: 1-877-898-0858). This site will give you the location of stores where tapioca pearls and straws can be purchased. You can also buy these items on the site, as well as get instructions on how to prepare the tapioca pearls.

Pineapple and Raspberry Obsession

This pineapple and raspberry smoothie, with more than a hint of rum, is seductively sweet. Whether enjoyed as a late-afternoon indulgence or as a light dessert, its flavors are deliciously addictive.

1 SERVING

3 tablespoons coconut rum
3 tablespoons dark rum
1 teaspoon honey, or to taste
1 cup partially frozen diced pineapple
½ cup partially frozen raspberries
¾ cup raspberry gelato or favorite raspberry, strawberry, or vanilla ice cream

Place all the ingredients in a blender and mix by using the on/off pulse function until the ingredients are mostly blended. Continue mixing, gradually increasing the speed, until the mixture is smooth. Pour the smoothie into a glass and garnish with a Pineapple Chip (page 231), if desired.

Raspberry and Pineapple Finale

If you're a raspberry devotee, you'll appreciate the intensity of raspberry flavors that dominate this sophisticated smoothie.

1 SERVING

3 tablespoons vodka
1 tablespoon raspberry liqueur
1 teaspoon honey
1 cup partially frozen diced pineapple
½ cup partially frozen raspberries
½ cup raspberry gelato or favorite raspberry,
     strawberry, or vanilla ice cream

Place all the ingredients in a blender and mix by using the on/off pulse function until the ingredients are mostly blended. Continue mixing, gradually increasing the speed, until the mixture is smooth. Pour the smoothie into a glass and garnish with Berries on a Skewer (page 212), if desired.

Sautéed Apple and Pear Devastation

Consider doubling or tripling the recipe so you always have a ready supply of this delectable apple filling on hand. One taste of this apple smoothie and you'll understand why.

1 SERVING

2 tablespoons (¼ stick) unsalted butter

1 cup peeled and cubed Golden Delicious apple

1 cup peeled and cubed pear

¼ teaspoon ground cinnamon

¼ teaspoon ground nutmeg

½ teaspoon pure vanilla extract

¼ cup apple juice

3 tablespoons Applejack brandy or
    other apple brandy

¾ cup caramel or favorite vanilla ice cream

Line a baking sheet with freezer paper. Set aside.

Melt the butter in a medium sauté pan over medium heat. Swirl the pan to coat evenly. Add the apple, pear, cinnamon, and nutmeg and blend well. Cook for 10 to 12 minutes, or until the fruits are tender, stirring occasionally. Add the vanilla and blend well. Remove the pan from the heat and place it on a cooling rack. When the apple and pear mixture is cool, transfer it to the prepared baking sheet and freeze for 1 hour or more.

When you are ready to make the smoothie, place the apple juice, apple brandy, apple and pear mixture, and ice cream in a blender and mix by using the on/off pulse function until the ingredients are mostly blended. Continue mixing, gradually increasing the speed, until the mixture is smooth. Pour the smoothie into a glass and garnish with a Pear Chip (page 229), if desired.

Snickers Smoothie

While the Snickers candy bar was introduced in 1930 and remains popular today, you will adore its new reincarnation as a smoothie cocktail.

1 SERVING

2 tablespoons vodka
2 tablespoons white crème de cacao
2 tablespoons brown crème de cacao
1 teaspoon Chocolate Syrup (page 191)
1 cup partially frozen diced banana
2 tablespoons creamy peanut butter
½ cup vanilla ice cream

Place all the ingredients in a blender and mix by using the on/off pulse function until the ingredients are mostly blended. Continue mixing, gradually increasing the speed, until the mixture is smooth. Pour the smoothie into a glass and garnish with a Peanut Butter–Chocolate Drop (page 227), if desired.

Spiced Pear Extravaganza

The wine and spices in this simple syrup enhance the flavor of the pear. Blended into a smoothie, it's the perfect complement to a macadamia brittle or cinnamon ice cream.

1 SERVING

¾ cup white wine

¼ cup sugar

1 3-inch cinnamon stick

1 whole clove

1 teaspoon pure vanilla extract

1 ½ cups peeled and cubed pear

½ cup macadamia brittle, cinnamon, or
     favorite vanilla ice cream

Place a strainer over a medium bowl. Line a baking sheet with freezer paper. Set aside.

Bring the wine, sugar, cinnamon stick, clove, and vanilla to a boil in a medium saucepan over medium heat. Add the pears and blend well. Simmer for 5 minutes, or until the pears are tender, stirring occasionally. Remove the pan from the heat and place it on a cooling rack. When the pear mixture is cool, transfer it to the strainer over the bowl (reserve the liquid). Remove and discard the spices. Place the pears on the prepared baking sheet and freeze for

RECIPE CONTINUES

1 hour or more. Cover the bowl containing the liquid and refrigerate.

When you are ready to make the smoothie, place the reserved liquid, pears, and ice cream in a blender and mix by using the on/off pulse function until the ingredients are mostly blended. Continue mixing, gradually increasing the speed, until the mixture is smooth. Pour the smoothie into a glass and garnish with a Pear Chip (page 176), if desired.

Strawberry Alexander

A Brandy Alexander is a sweet drink traditionally served after dinner. Gussied up with strawberries and ice cream, this smoothie morphs
into a sublime dessert or sexy after-dinner
drink.

1 SERVING

2 tablespoons brandy
2 tablespoons white crème de cacao
1 ½ cups partially frozen diced strawberries
½ cup vanilla ice cream

Place all the ingredients in a blender and mix by
using the on/off pulse function until the ingredients
are mostly blended. Continue mixing, gradually
increasing the speed, until the mixture is smooth.
Pour the smoothie into a glass and garnish with a
Strawberry Fan (page 233), if desired.

Strawberry Bellini

A Bellini is traditionally made with peaches and champagne. Substituting strawberries for peaches adds a new dimension to this smoothie version of the popular cocktail.

1 SERVING

6 tablespoons Asti Spumante or
    other sweet sparkling wine
1 tablespoon white rum
1 tablespoon vodka
1 teaspoon honey, or to taste
1 ½ cups partially frozen diced strawberries
½ cup strawberry sorbet

Place all the ingredients in a blender and mix by using the on/off pulse function until the ingredients are mostly blended. Continue mixing, gradually increasing the speed, until the mixture is smooth. Pour the smoothie into a glass and garnish with a Strawberry Fan (page 233), if desired.

Tiramisù

Tiramisù, originally known as *zuppa de duca* (the Duke's soup), is a luscious dessert created in Tuscany in honor of the eighteenth-century visit of Grand Duke Cosimode Medici III. Rumor has it that when the dessert was introduced in Venice, the city's courtesans used it as a pick-me-up (translation of tiramisù) to fortify themselves between amorous encounters. Follow their example or find your own excuse for pampering yourself with a glassful of this Tuscan delight.

1 SERVING

¼ cup chilled espresso or strong coffee

2 tablespoons Kahlúa or other coffee liqueur

2 tablespoons mascarpone cheese,
    at room temperature

1 cup partially frozen diced banana

½ cup coffee gelato or favorite coffee ice cream

Place all the ingredients in a blender and mix by using the on/off pulse function until the ingredients are mostly blended. Continue mixing, gradually increasing the speed, until the mixture is smooth. Pour the smoothie into a glass and garnish with a Vanilla Pirouette (page 213), if desired.

6

Sinful Sauces and Toppings

Beyond Chocolate Fudge

Caramels are only a fad.
Chocolate is a permanent thing.

—MILTON SNAVELY HERSHEY
(1857–1945)
founder of the Hershey Chocolate Company

IF YOU'RE LOOKING TO ADD A LITTLE CULINARY mischief to your life, then look no further than this collection of tempting sauces and toppings. You'll adore how a divinely luxurious chocolate syrup or a rich and gooey caramel sauce can elevate an ordinary fruit-filled smoothie to a sensual delight. Imagine the ecstasy when you luxuriate in the taste of a smoothie made with peaches smothered in caramel, bananas cloaked in chocolate, or pineapple seeped in a praline sauce. Are you tempted yet? With these sumptuous sauces and toppings, smoothiedom has entered a new era.

Butterscotch Sauce

The unique flavor of butterscotch comes from its blend of butter and brown sugar. When it is added to a smoothie, none of its signature essence is lost. You'll adore it in the Banana, Butterscotch, and Macadamia Nut Supreme (page 89)!

1 CUP

4 tablespoons (½ stick) unsalted butter
6 tablespoons light corn syrup
¼ cup granulated sugar
¼ cup firmly packed dark brown sugar
6 tablespoons heavy cream

Melt the butter in a heavy medium skillet over low heat. Add the corn syrup and sugars and blend. Increase the heat to medium-high and bring the mixture to a boil. Continue boiling without stirring for 2 minutes. Remove the saucepan from the heat. Using a wire whisk with a long handle, gradually whisk in the heavy cream. Allow the sauce to come to room temperature. When the Butterscotch Sauce is cool, transfer it to a covered container and refrigerate for up to 4 weeks. (After the sauce has been refrigerated, it may be necessary to return it to its original consistency by heating it in the microwave for a minute or two.)

Caramel Sauce

Similar to its butterscotch cousin, this sauce is rich, gooey, and over-the-top. It's fabulous when added to a smoothie, but it also makes a delectable companion to other frozen desserts. One of my favorite smoothies made with this sinfully rich sauce is Berries and Caramel Mania (page 96).

1 ³/₄ CUPS

1 ¼ cups sugar
6 tablespoons cold water
¾ teaspoon cream of tartar
¾ cup heavy cream
4 tablespoons (½ stick) unsalted butter,
   at room temperature and cut into 8 pieces
¾ teaspoon pure vanilla extract
Dash of coarse salt

Combine the sugar, water, and cream of tartar in a heavy medium saucepan over medium heat. Cook for 5 minutes, stirring occasionally with a wooden spoon to dissolve the sugar and brushing down the sugar on the sides of the pan to prevent it from crystallizing. Increase the heat to medium-high and bring the mixture to a boil. Continue boiling without stirring for 5 to 7 minutes, or until the mixture turns amber or pale golden in color, swirling the pan occasionally.

Remove the saucepan from the heat. Using a wire whisk with a long handle, gradually add the heavy cream (the mixture will boil rapidly) and stir until smooth. Add the butter and whisk until melted, then add the vanilla and salt; blend well. Allow the sauce to come to room temperature. When the Caramel Sauce is cool, transfer it to a covered container and refrigerate for up to 4 weeks.

Chocolate, Caramel, and Peanut Butter Sauce

This sauce is a celebration of three of our favorite indulgences: chocolate, caramel, and peanut butter. For a real fantasy come true, you must sample the Banana, Peanut Butter, and Chocolate Ecstasy smoothie (page 94).

³/₄ CUP

¼ cup Chocolate Sauce (page 190)
¼ cup Caramel Sauce (page 182)
¼ cup heavy cream
2 tablespoons creamy peanut butter

Combine the Chocolate Sauce, Caramel Sauce, and heavy cream in a heavy small saucepan over medium-high heat. Bring to a boil, stirring occasionally with a wire whisk. Lower the heat to medium and simmer for 5 minutes. Remove the saucepan from the heat and add the peanut butter; blend well. Allow the sauce to come to room temperature. When the Chocolate, Caramel, and Peanut Butter Sauce is cool, transfer it to a covered container and refrigerate for up to 4 weeks. (After the sauce has been refrigerated, it may be necessary to return it to its original consistency by heating it in the microwave for a minute or two.)

Chocolate Coconut Sauce

It's hard to believe that a small amount of coconut extract can add such an incredible flavor to chocolate. After one taste of the Chocolate Coconut Island Breeze smoothie (page 101), I think you'll agree.

²/₃ CUP

²/₃ cup Chocolate Sauce (page 190)
1 teaspoon coconut extract

Combine the Chocolate Sauce and coconut extract in a small bowl. Transfer the Chocolate Coconut Sauce to a covered container and refrigerate for up to 4 weeks. (After the sauce has been refrigerated, it may be necessary to return it to its original consistency by heating it in the microwave for a minute or two.)

Chocolate Crunch

This luscious Chocolate Crunch is easy to prepare and makes the perfect partner to mix into a smoothie or spoon into the bottom of a glass. It can also be used as a topping over any of the sinful delights celebrated in this book, such as the Cherry Extravaganza smoothie (page 38).

2 CUPS

1 cup slivered almonds
1 cup (6 ounces) semisweet chocolate chips
1 teaspoon vegetable shortening
1 cup cornflakes

Preheat the oven to 350°F. Line a baking sheet with nonstick aluminum foil. Set aside.

Place the almonds in a single layer in a shallow pan and bake for 10 to 15 minutes, or until golden brown and fragrant.

Place the chocolate chips and vegetable shortening in a heavy medium saucepan over low heat. Cover and cook until the chocolate melts, stirring occasionally. Add the slivered almonds and cornflakes and blend well.

Using a metal spatula, spread the chocolate mixture into a 7-inch square (it does not have to be exact) on the prepared baking sheet. Freeze the chocolate mixture for 15 minutes. Remove the baking sheet from the freezer and transfer the chocolate mixture to a heavy resealable bag; seal the bag (make sure to get the air out of the bag). Using a mallet or blunt object, gently pound the mixture within the sealed bag until it is broken into small pieces. The Chocolate Crunch can be kept in an air-tight container in the refrigerator for up to 2 months or in the freezer for 6 months.

Chocolate, Nut, and Raisin Crunch

You'll adore this versatile Chocolate, Nut, and Raisin Crunch. It is heavenly tasting when crushed and either sprinkled on top or mixed into a smoothie. Try the delicious Pineapple and Raspberry Crunch Smoothie (page 120) and I think you'll agree. The crunch can also be broken into shards and used as a garnish by inserting a piece upright into the top of a smoothie.

1 ¹/₂ CUPS

4 ounces white (or semisweet) chocolate,
    coarsely chopped
¼ cup salted peanuts
¼ cup raisins

Line a baking sheet with nonstick aluminum foil. Set aside.

Place the chocolate in a heavy small saucepan over low heat. Cover and cook, stirring occasionally, for 12 to 15 minutes, or until the chocolate has melted. Add the peanuts and raisins and blend well.

Using a metal spatula, spread the chocolate mixture into a rectangle, approximately 6 x 5 inches (the mixture will be about ½ inch thick), on the prepared baking sheet. Freeze the chocolate mixture for 15 minutes. Remove the baking sheet from the freezer and transfer the chocolate mixture to a heavy resealable bag; seal the bag (make sure to get the air out of the bag). Using a mallet or blunt object, gently pound the mixture within the sealed bag until it is broken into small pieces. The Chocolate, Nut, and Raisin Crunch can be kept in an airtight container in the freezer for up to a month.

Chocolate Sauce

Beware: This sauce is a chocoholic's temptation.
Try this dense and sinfully rich Chocolate Sauce
in a Chocolate-Covered Halvah Smoothie (page
102) and you'll find yourself dreaming up ways
to use it over and over again.

¾ CUP

2 tablespoons light corn syrup
2 tablespoons heavy cream
1 tablespoon canola oil
4 ounces (4 squares) semisweet chocolate,
    finely chopped
½ teaspoon pure vanilla extract
2 tablespoons milk

Place the corn syrup, 1 tablespoon heavy cream, and
the oil in a heavy medium saucepan over medium-
high heat and bring to a boil, stirring occasionally.
Remove the saucepan from the heat. Using a wire
whisk, add the chocolate and vanilla and stir until
smooth. Gradually add the milk and remaining
1 tablespoon heavy cream and blend well. Allow the
sauce to come to room temperature. When the
Chocolate Sauce is cool, transfer it to a covered container and refrigerate for up to 4 weeks. (After the
sauce has been refrigerated, it may be necessary to
return it to its original consistency by heating it in
the microwave for a minute or two.)

Chocolate Syrup

Although many commercially made chocolate syrups are available, I prefer to make my own. This recipe is very easy to prepare, and the flavor has just the right amount of chocolate essence. In fact, you'll swoon over the Mint Oreo and Chocolate Decadence smoothie (page 111)—the name says it all.

³/₄ CUP

⅓ cup Dutch-processed cocoa
3 tablespoons white corn syrup
¼ cup boiling water
¼ cup sugar
½ teaspoon pure vanilla extract
Dash of coarse salt

Combine the cocoa and corn syrup in a heavy small saucepan over low heat. Using a wire whisk, add the boiling water and blend well. Cook for 3 minutes, stirring occasionally. Whisk in the sugar, then add the vanilla and salt; blend well. Remove the saucepan from the heat and allow the syrup to come to room temperature. When the Chocolate Syrup is cool, transfer it to a covered container and refrigerate for up to 4 weeks.

German Chocolate Sauce

Combining German and semisweet chocolate makes a rich and luscious sauce. Added to a smoothie, such as the German Chocolate Smoothie (page 107), it results in a heart-stopping treat.

1 CUP

2 ounces (½ bar) German sweet chocolate,
    coarsely chopped
2 ounces (2 squares) semisweet chocolate,
    coarsely chopped
½ cup sugar
½ cup light or heavy cream

Melt the chocolates in a double boiler, stirring occasionally. Add the sugar and ¼ cup of the cream and stir until blended. Add the remaining ¼ cup of cream and blend well. Remove the saucepan from the heat and allow the sauce to come to room temperature. When the German Chocolate Sauce is cool, transfer it to a covered container and refrigerate for up to 4 weeks. (After the sauce has been refrigerated, it may be necessary to return it to its original consistency by heating it in the microwave for a minute or two.)

Macadamia Nut Praline Crunch

Most macadamia nuts are produced in Hawaii, but they are actually native to Australia. Although probably known to the indigenous people of that continent for centuries, the macadamia was first described botanically by Baron Ferdinand von Muller, an Australian botanist who named it in honor of his good friend from Scotland, Dr. John Macadam. I think you'll agree that when macadamia nuts are toasted, made into a praline crunch, and blended into a smoothie, such as the Pineapple, Caramel, and Macadamia Nut Orgy (page 122), the end result is deliriously rich and delicious.

¾ CUP

¾ cup cold water
6 tablespoons sugar
Heaping ½ cup coarsely chopped toasted
    macadamia nuts (see Note)

Line a baking sheet with nonstick aluminum foil. Set aside.

Place the water and sugar in a heavy medium skillet over medium-high heat and bring to a boil. When the sugar begins to caramelize, stir well. Con-

RECIPE CONTINUES

tinue boiling, swirling the saucepan occasionally, for 8 to 15 minutes, or until the sugar turns a deep amber color. Add the macadamia nuts and blend with a wooden spoon to coat the nuts evenly. Immediately pour the macadamia nut mixture on the prepared baking sheet and use a wooden spoon to spread it in a thin layer. Allow the mixture to cool for 30 minutes. When the macadamia nut mixture is cool, place it in a heavy resealable bag; seal the bag (make sure to get the air out of the bag). Using a mallet or blunt object, gently pound the mixture within the sealed bag until it is broken into small pieces. The Macadamia Nut Praline Crunch can be kept in an airtight container in the refrigerator for up to 2 months or in the freezer for 6 months.

NOTE: To toast macadamia nuts, place them in a single layer in a pan and bake in a preheated 400°F. oven for 5 to 8 minutes, or until golden brown and fragrant.

Milk Chocolate and Peanut Crunch

I don't know about you, but I can't resist anything made with milk chocolate. When you add peanuts, the combination becomes addictive. You'll agree that this crunch is positively sublime mixed into a smoothie, after sampling the deliriously delectable Banana, Peanut Butter, and Milk Chocolate Explosion (page 95). Or, for an over-the-top experience, sprinkle the crunch on top or spoon it into the bottom of a glass filled with a Chocolate Malt Smoothie (page 103).

1 ½ CUPS

1 cup milk chocolate chips
   (or 1 7-ounce milk chocolate bar)
⅔ cup salted peanuts

Line a baking sheet with nonstick aluminum foil. Set aside.

Place the chocolate in a heavy small saucepan over low heat. Cover and cook, stirring occasionally, for 10 to 12 minutes, or until the chocolate has melted. Add the peanuts and blend well.

Using a metal spatula, spread the chocolate mixture into a 6- or 7-inch square (it does not have to

RECIPE CONTINUES

be exact) on the prepared baking sheet. Freeze the chocolate mixture for 15 minutes. Remove the baking sheet from the freezer and transfer the chocolate mixture to a heavy resealable bag; seal the bag (make sure to get the air out of the bag). Using a mallet or blunt object, gently pound the mixture within the sealed bag until it is broken into small pieces. The Milk Chocolate and Peanut Crunch can be kept in an airtight container in the freezer for up to a month.

Milk Chocolate Sauce

How can anything this simple to prepare taste so drop-dead delicious? If you obsess over milk chocolate like I do, then you'll adore this sauce. It's heavenly spooned into the bottom of a glass or swirled into a smoothie to give it extra naughtiness. Not convinced? Wait until you taste an Almond Joy Smoothie (page 83)—it's nirvana.

³/₄ CUP

1 cup milk chocolate chips
(or 1 7-ounce milk chocolate bar)
⅓ cup very hot water

Place the chocolate in a heavy small saucepan over low heat. Cover and cook, stirring occasionally, for 10 to 12 minutes, or until the chocolate has melted. Using a wire whisk, add the water and blend well. Remove the saucepan from the heat and allow the sauce to come to room temperature. When the Milk Chocolate Sauce is cool, transfer it to a covered container and refrigerate for up to 4 weeks. (After the sauce has been refrigerated, it may be necessary to return it to its original consistency by heating it in the microwave for a minute or two.)

Pastry Crunch

For many of us, the favorite part of any pie is the piecrust. This Pastry Crunch is a close cousin to piecrust, and when used as a topping or mixed into many of the smoothies that are similar to cobblers and pies, it adds a rich flavor and an interesting texture. You can appreciate the essence of this flavorful crunch in an Apple Pie à la Mode smoothie (page 25).

2¼ CUPS

1 cup flour
½ cup (1 stick) unsalted butter, cut into small pieces
½ cup chopped pecans or walnuts
¼ cup sugar

Preheat the oven to 250°F. Line a rimmed baking sheet with parchment paper. Set aside.

Using a pastry blender or 2 knives, combine all the ingredients in a medium bowl until it resembles oatmeal. Transfer the mixture to the prepared baking sheet and bake for 1 hour, stirring every 15 minutes. Remove the baking sheet from the oven and place it on a cooling rack. When the Pastry Crunch is cool, transfer it to an airtight container and place in the freezer for up to 4 months.

Pecan Praline Crunch

This recipe can also be made with slivered almonds, walnuts, or toasted hazelnuts in place of pecans. You'll adore the essence of pecan pralines in the temptingly delicious Pineapple, Banana, and Praline Temptation smoothie (page 121).

³/₄ CUP

³/₄ cup coarsely chopped pecans
  (or slivered almonds, walnuts, or hazelnuts; see Note)
½ cup sugar
¼ cup cold water
⅛ teaspoon cream of tartar

Preheat the oven to 350°F. Line a baking sheet with nonstick aluminum foil. Set aside.

Place the pecans in a single layer in a shallow pan and bake for 10 minutes. Remove the pan from the oven and place it on a cooling rack.

Place the sugar, water, and cream of tartar in a heavy medium skillet over medium heat, stirring occasionally, for 4 to 6 minutes, or until the sugar begins to dissolve. Raise the heat to medium-high and cook, stirring occasionally, for 6 to 8 minutes, or until the sugar turns a deep amber color. Add the pecans and blend with a wooden spoon to coat the nuts evenly. Immediately pour the pecan mixture on

RECIPE CONTINUES

the prepared baking sheet and use a wooden spoon to spread it in a thin layer. Allow the mixture to cool for 30 minutes. When the pecan mixture is cool, place it in a heavy resealable bag; seal the bag (make sure to get the air out of the bag). Using a mallet or blunt object, gently pound the mixture within the sealed bag until it is broken into small pieces. The Pecan Praline Crunch can be kept in an airtight container in the refrigerator for up to 2 months or in the freezer for 6 months.

NOTE: To toast hazelnuts, place them in a single layer in a pan and bake in a preheated 350°F. oven for 10 to 15 minutes, or until golden brown and fragrant.

Pine Nut Brittle

Brittle is made of caramelized sugar that is spread in a thin sheet to cool. It's often made with pecans, but it gains new credentials when made with pine nuts. Try the Pine Nut Pear-adise smoothie (page 66) for a unique taste temptation.

2 CUPS

1 cup pine nuts
1½ teaspoons unsalted butter, cut into small pieces
¼ teaspoon coarse salt
1 cup sugar
⅓ cup cold water

Line a baking sheet with nonstick aluminum paper. Set aside.

Place the pine nuts, butter, and salt in a small bowl and blend.

Place the sugar and water in a heavy medium skillet over medium heat, stirring occasionally, for 4 to 6 minutes, or until the sugar begins to dissolve. Raise the heat to medium-high and cook for 7 to 10 minutes, or until the sugar turns a deep amber color, swirling the pan occasionally. Add the pine nut mixture and blend with a wooden spoon to coat the pine nuts evenly. Immediately pour the pine nut mixture on the prepared baking sheet and use a wooden

RECIPE CONTINUES

spoon to spread it in a thin layer. Allow the mixture to cool for 30 minutes. When the pine nut mixture is cool, place it in a heavy resealable bag; seal the bag (make sure to get the air out of the bag). Using a mallet or blunt object, gently pound the mixture within the sealed bag until it is broken into small pieces. The Pine Nut Brittle can be kept in an airtight container in the refrigerator for up to 2 months or in the freezer for 6 months.

NOTE: For a more robust flavor, the pine nuts can be toasted before they are added to the caramelized sugar mixture. Place the pine nuts in a single layer in a pan and bake in a preheated 350°F. oven for 10 to 15 minutes, or until golden brown and fragrant.

Praline Sauce

This wonderful Praline Sauce will turn any smoothie into a southern delight. For an Alabama experience, try the Peach and Praline Indulgence smoothie (page 115).

³/₄ CUP

½ cup sugar

¼ cup buttermilk

½ tablespoon molasses

2 tablespoons (¼ stick) unsalted butter

2½ teaspoons white corn syrup

¼ teaspoon baking soda

¼ cup or more chopped pecans

½ teaspoon pure vanilla extract

Combine the sugar, buttermilk, molasses, butter, corn syrup, and baking soda in a heavy medium saucepan over medium heat and bring to a gentle boil. Reduce the heat and simmer, stirring occasionally, for 10 minutes. Remove the saucepan from the heat and add the pecans and vanilla; blend well. Allow the sauce to come to room temperature. When the Praline Sauce is cool, transfer it to a covered container and refrigerate for up to 4 weeks. (After the sauce has been refrigerated, it may be necessary to return it to its original consistency by heating it in the microwave for a minute or two.)

Raspberry Sauce

Once you taste this delectable Raspberry Sauce, you'll discover how easy it is to transform a humble smoothie into a classy showstopper. Whether blended with other smoothie ingredients, spooned in the bottom of a glass, or drizzled over the top, it adds a certain razzle-dazzle that is certain to impress. Maybe this is how the Razzle-Dazzle Raspberry, Blueberry, and Strawberry Smoothie (page 69) got its name.

¹/₂ CUP

½ pint (1 cup) raspberries
2 tablespoons sugar
½ tablespoon fresh lemon juice

Place the raspberries in the workbowl of a food processor fitted with a metal blade and process until puréed. Transfer the puréed raspberries to a wire sieve placed over a heavy small saucepan. Using a rubber spatula or the back of a spoon, press down on the raspberries to release as much raspberry liquid as possible. Remove the sieve and discard the seeds. Add the sugar and lemon juice to the raspberry liquid and blend well. Cook over low heat for 10 minutes, or until the raspberry sauce is hot. Remove the saucepan from the heat. Allow the sauce to come to room temperature. When the Raspberry Sauce is cool, transfer it to a covered container and refrigerate for up to 1 week.

South-of-the-Border Chocolate Sauce

There is something extraordinarily tempting about a chocolate sauce made with cinnamon and orange juice. Its wonderful flavors will remain intact when you add it to the South-of-the-Border Sundae (page 125), endowing the smoothie with a wonderfully rich and spicy essence.

1 CUP

2 tablespoons unsweetened cocoa
¼ teaspoon cornstarch
⅛ teaspoon ground cinnamon
¼ cup fresh orange juice
½ cup Chocolate Syrup (page 191)

Combine the cocoa, cornstarch, and cinnamon in a small saucepan over medium heat. Whisk in the orange juice and blend well. Cook, stirring frequently, for 4 to 5 minutes, or until the mixture begins to bubble. Add the Chocolate Syrup and blend well. Remove the saucepan from the heat and allow the sauce to come to room temperature. When the South-of-the-Border Chocolate Sauce is cool, transfer it to a covered container and refrigerate for up to 4 weeks. (After the sauce has been refrigerated, it may be necessary to return it to its original consistency by heating it in the microwave for a minute or two.)

Sugar's Hot Fudge Sauce

Every holiday, my friend Sugar gives me a jar of this absolutely sensational hot fudge sauce. You can serve it on almost any sweet, but it's exceptionally delightful when combined with other smoothie ingredients. You'll especially appreciate how well this sauce marries with coffee in the Caffé Speciale smoothie (page 98).

2 1/4 CUPS

4 ounces (1 stick) unsalted butter
3 ounces (3 squares) unsweetened chocolate,
    coarsely chopped
1½ cups sugar
¼ teaspoon coarse salt
6 ounces evaporated milk
2½ tablespoons cold water

Place the butter and chocolate in a heavy large saucepan over low heat. Cover and cook, stirring occasionally, until the chocolate has melted. Using a wire whisk, slowly add the sugar and salt and blend well. Gradually add the evaporated milk and water, stirring until smooth. Cook for 25 to 30 minutes, or until the hot fudge sauce thickens slightly. (The sauce will thicken more as it cools.) Remove the saucepan from the heat and allow the sauce to come to room temperature. When Sugar's Hot Fudge

Sauce is cool, transfer it to a covered container and refrigerate for up to 4 weeks. (After the sauce has been refrigerated, it may be necessary to return it to its original consistency by heating it in the microwave for a minute or two.)

$$\mathcal{7}$$

Great Garnishes

Go to the Head of the Glass

Garnishes must be matched like a tie to a suit.

—FERNAND POINT (1897–1955)
Ma Gastronomie

SMOOTHIES HAVE TRADITIONALLY BEEN KNOWN more for their unique combination of flavors and textures than for their appearance. But when trying to reinvent a smoothie as a seductive cocktail or dessert, a well-chosen garnish can magically create something visually grand out of an otherwise simple combination of ingredients. Whether you choose a basic garnish, such as Berries on a Skewer, or a more elaborate embellishment, such as a Cinnamon Pirouette, to adorn your smoothie, the added colors and shapes can result in an impressive creation that is striking in appearance. What's more, most of these garnishes are exceptionally delicious themselves.

In this chapter, you will find a host of novel ideas for creating garnishes to add a sublimely decadent touch to your sinful smoothies. Most are not very complicated to make. You can choose to make many garnishes well in advance, and some can even be kept frozen, so you can have a ready supply available for an instant smoothie celebration.

On the other hand, if you don't have the time or inclination to make your own garnishes, consider picking up some fun accessories at your neighborhood party store, such as multicolored and uniquely shaped straws, cocktail umbrellas, brightly colored metallic sparklers, paper flowers, or fancy swizzle sticks. In addition, a number of edible accessories are available on the Internet, such as chocolate-lined vanilla or strawberry-flavored cookie straws or cookie spoons, made of plain or chocolate-dipped edible cookies (these items are available at www.yohay.com; unfortunately, this company requires a minimum order of three cases). The cookie spoons are also available at www.garden ofinspirations.com. In the left column on this screen, scroll down and select "Munchies." On the next screen, choose "Cookies Selection" to find the cookie spoons.

While it's true that a sinful smoothie is inherently seductive and appealing, I am convinced that once you've served one artfully decorated with a colorful and tasty embellishment, you'll agree that this added touch will make its siren song, beckoning you and your guests into gastronomic ecstasy, even more irresistible.

Apple Chips

Apple Chips are crunchy, paper-thin slices of apples. They are the perfect garnish to dress up any smoothie. Not only do they add a sophisticated elegance to smoothies or other desserts, but they are delicious as well. The chips are best when the apples are thinly sliced with a mandoline or vegetable slicer; however, with a little patience, a sharp knife can be just as effective.

16 to 20 CHIPS

1 Granny Smith or Golden Delicious apple,
    unpeeled and uncored
4 cups cold water
$\frac{1}{4}$ cup fresh lemon juice
2 cups sugar

Preheat the oven to 200°F. Line a baking sheet with parchment paper or a silicone baking mat. Set aside.

Thinly slice the apples into horizontal rings about $\frac{1}{16}$ inch thick or as thin as possible (remove and discard any seeds). Place the apple rings in a bowl filled with 2 cups of the water and 2 tablespoons of the lemon juice. Set aside.

Bring the sugar and the remaining 2 cups water and 2 tablespoons lemon juice to a boil in a large saucepan over medium-high heat, stirring frequently to dissolve the sugar. Add the apple rings, one at a time, and cook for 1 to 2 minutes, or until the mixture returns to a boil.

Using tongs, remove the apple rings from the mixture and place them in a single layer on the prepared baking sheet. Pat the rings dry with a double layer of paper towels. Bake the apple rings for 1 hour, or until they are dry and crisp. (To test for doneness, remove an apple ring from the baking sheet and allow it to cool. If it is not crisp, bake the apple rings a little longer, checking every 15 minutes to see if they're done.) Remove the Apple Chips from the baking sheet and place them on a wire rack to cool completely. The Apple Chips can be stored in an airtight container in a cool, dry place for up to 2 days.

Berries on a Skewer

This beautiful yet easy-to-prepare garnish adds a rich color to most smoothies.

2 SKEWERS OF BERRIES

½ cup fresh raspberries, blueberries, or blackberries
2 6- to 10-inch wooden skewers

Thread 5 to 6 berries of your choice onto the upper half of each skewer. Be sure to use skewers that are long enough to allow the bottom piece of fruit to rest comfortably on the rim of the glass. Refrigerate in an airtight container for up to 2 hours.

Chocolate, Cinnamon, or Vanilla Pirouettes

Garnishing with a pirouette cookie is a delicious way to adorn many smoothies. Although there are a host of commercially made pirouettes that are available in assorted sizes and flavors, I prefer to make my own. The recipe for these cookies is so versatile, you can choose the flavor that most appeals to you.

6 TO 7 PIROUETTES

3 tablespoons flour

1 heaping tablespoon Dutch-processed cocoa for Chocolate Pirouettes, 1 teaspoon ground cinnamon for Cinnamon Pirouettes, or ¼ teaspoon pure vanilla extract for Vanilla Pirouettes

2 tablespoons (¼ stick) unsalted butter, at room temperature

¼ cup confectioners' sugar

1 large egg white

Preheat the oven to 350°F. Line a baking sheet with a silicone mat or parchment paper lightly coated with a nonstick vegetable spray. Set aside.

TO MAKE CHOCOLATE PIROUETTES:
Combine the flour and cocoa in a small bowl and blend well.

RECIPE CONTINUES

Place the butter and confectioners' sugar in a tall medium bowl and beat with a handheld electric mixer (or an electric mixer) on low speed for 1 to 2 minutes, or until creamy. Add half the cocoa mixture and beat on low speed until blended. Add the egg white and remaining cocoa mixture and beat just until incorporated.

Spoon a heaping tablespoon of batter on each half of the prepared baking sheet. Using an angular metal spatula (or straight metal spatula), spread the batter into a 5-inch circle, making sure the batter is thin but not transparent. (Don't worry if the batter looks uneven—it will even out during the baking process.) Bake for 8 minutes, or until set. Remove the baking sheet from the oven and use a metal spatula to loosen each cookie. Using your fingers, quickly roll up the cookie into a tight cylinder or cigar shape. Place the cookies, seam-side down, on a cake rack to cool completely. Allow the baking sheet to cool completely before repeating the process with the remaining batter. The cookies can be stored in an airtight container at room temperature or in the refrigerator for up to 1 week or frozen for several weeks.

TO MAKE CINNAMON PIROUETTES:
Follow the instructions for making Chocolate Pirouettes, with one exception: Add cinnamon instead of cocoa to the flour.

TO MAKE VANILLA PIROUETTES:
Follow the instructions for making Chocolate Pirouettes, with one exception: Do not add cocoa to the flour. Add vanilla to the egg white (not to the flour).

Chocolate-Covered Oreo Cookies

Who doesn't love Oreo cookies? Well, just imagine these sublime treats made extra sinful with a thick layer of chocolate. To make them even more appealing, you can cover the melted chocolate with chocolate sprinkles, edible confetti, or nonpareils, or you can dress them up by drizzling melted white chocolate all over. Best of all, they can be kept frozen for up to three months, so you can have a ready supply when you're feeling particularly daring.

16 TO 20 OREOS

16 to 20 double-filled Oreo cookies or
    favorite chocolate sandwich cookies (see Note)
16 to 20 10-inch wooden skewers
1 7-ounce milk chocolate bar, chopped
    (or semisweet or milk chocolate chips)
1 tablespoon vegetable shortening
1 cup chocolate sprinkles, edible confetti, or
    nonpareils (optional)

Hold each cookie tightly between your fingers and insert a wooden skewer halfway into the white filling of each, being careful to keep the cookie intact.

RECIPE CONTINUES

Place them on a baking sheet lined with nonstick aluminum foil and freeze for 1 hour.

When you are ready to prepare the Oreo cookies, melt the chocolate and vegetable shortening in a heavy small saucepan, covered, over low heat, stirring occasionally. Once the chocolate has melted, remove the saucepan from the heat and tilt it at about a 45-degree angle to facilitate the dipping process. Holding onto the skewer, dip each cookie into the chocolate, allowing the excess to drip back into the saucepan while gently twisting the skewer. Immediately place the cookie in the optional chocolate sprinkles, edible confetti, or nonpareils and coat both sides (or just one side).

Place the skewers upright in a glass to allow the chocolate to harden. The cookies can be used to garnish a smoothie once the chocolate has set. If the cookies are not going to be used immediately, place them on a baking sheet lined with parchment paper or nonstick aluminum foil and freeze for 15 minutes, then wrap each one tightly in plastic wrap. Freeze for up to 3 months. Allow the cookies to sit at room temperature for at least 10 minutes before serving, then place upright in a smoothie.

NOTE: The recipe can be made with mint Oreo cookies. Also, the recipe can be cut in half.

Chocolate-Dipped Frozen Baby Bananas

Baby bananas are native to tropical countries such as Central and South America. They are shaped like miniature slender bananas and are very sweet. When dipped in chocolate and gussied up with a topping, these sumptuous garnishes add pizzazz and great taste to any smoothie.

8 BABY BANANAS

8 6- to 10-inch wooden skewers or lollipop sticks
8 baby bananas
    (or 2 to 3 bananas cut into 1-inch chunks), peeled
1 7-ounce milk chocolate bar, chopped
    (or 1 cup semisweet or milk chocolate chips)
1 tablespoon vegetable shortening
1 cup either edible confetti, chocolate sprinkles,
    coconut (toasted, if desired), nonpareils, or
    chopped peanuts (optional)

Insert a wooden skewer halfway into each baby banana or banana chunk. Place them on a baking sheet lined with nonstick aluminum foil or freezer paper and freeze for 1 hour.

When you are ready to prepare the baby bananas, melt the chocolate and vegetable shorten-

RECIPE CONTINUES

ing in a heavy small saucepan, covered, over low heat, stirring occasionally. Once the chocolate has melted, remove the saucepan from the heat and tilt it at about a 45-degree angle to facilitate the dipping process. Holding onto the skewer, dip each banana into the chocolate, allowing the excess to drip back into the saucepan while gently twisting the skewers. (Do this step quickly because the cold banana will set the chocolate.) Immediately roll the banana in the optional edible confetti, chocolate sprinkles, coconut, nonpareils, or peanuts.

There are several ways to allow the chocolate to set on the dipped baby bananas. You can insert the skewers upright into Oasis (a green spongelike material used in plant nurseries) or a piece of Styrofoam, which will act as an anchor for them. Or they can be placed in a pan lined with nonstick aluminum foil or upright in a glass.

When the chocolate has set, freeze the baby bananas for 2 hours or overnight. Once the baby bananas are frozen, wrap each one tightly in plastic wrap and keep in the freezer for up to 5 days. Allow the bananas to sit at room temperature for at least 10 minutes before serving, then place upright in a smoothie.

Cinnamon and Sugar Twists

For a whimsical and delicious touch, insert one to two Cinnamon and Sugar Twists upright in a smoothie. These delectable twists, if made in advance and stored in the freezer, can be served directly without thawing but are equally delicious when served at room temperature.

14 TWISTS

3 tablespoons sugar

¼ teaspoon ground cinnamon

½ (17.3 ounce) package Pepperidge Farm pastry sheets (1 sheet)

Flour, for dusting

1 small egg white, beaten until foamy

Line a baking sheet with parchment paper (this sheet will be used to refrigerate the dough). Next, place two baking sheets on top of each other and line the top one with parchment paper. (Placing two sheets on top of each other will result in more even heat when baking the twists. However, if you have only one sheet, it will work almost as well.)

Combine the sugar and cinnamon in a small bowl and blend well.

Thaw the pastry sheet at room temperature for 30 minutes, then cut in half. Rewrap one half in plastic wrap and return to freezer. Wrap the remaining pastry sheet half in plastic wrap and allow it to sit in the refrigerator for several hours or overnight.

RECIPE CONTINUES

Lightly dust a sheet of parchment paper with flour. Unfold the thawed pastry sheet (it should measure approximately 5 x 9 inches) and place it on the paper. Turn to coat both sides in the flour. Refold the pastry sheet (it should now measure 3½ x 5 inches) and place a piece of parchment paper on top. Using a rolling pin, flatten the pastry sheet into a 6-inch square (it does not have to be exact).

Brush the bottom half lightly with the beaten egg white and sprinkle the cinnamon mixture over the egg white within ½ inch of the edges. Fold the top half (or side without any egg white and cinnamon mixture) over and press the edges together. Place a piece of parchment paper on top of the pastry sheet and roll it into an 8 x 10-inch rectangle. Leave the parchment on top of the pastry sheet and place it on the prepared single baking sheet. Refrigerate for 1 hour.

Preheat the oven to 375°F. When the pastry sheet is firm, remove the parchment paper. Using a pizza cutter or sharp knife, cut the sheet crosswise into ¼-inch strips. Working with 1 strip at a time, start in the center and work toward the end, twisting the dough in opposite directions until the strip looks like a long spiral. Trim the ends. Place each strip on the parchment-paper surface of the prepared doubled baking sheets, 1 inch apart. Press the ends down slightly to prevent the twists from curling up. Bake for 17 to 20 minutes, or until golden brown. Remove the baking sheet from the oven and place it on a cooling rack. After 5 minutes, loosen the twists from the sheet. When the Cinnamon and Sugar twists are cool, they can be stored in an airtight container or resealable plastic bag in the freezer for several weeks or at room temperature for up to 1 week.

Cinnamon- or Chocolate-Dipped Tortilla Triangles

These triangles are so delicious you might want to make extra. With or without the chocolate, the triangles are fabulous as a garnish, an accompaniment to coffee, or a snack.

8 TORTILLA TRIANGLES

2 tablespoons (¼ stick) unsalted butter
1 tablespoon firmly packed dark brown sugar
1 teaspoon ground cinnamon
1 8-inch flour tortilla
2 ounces (2 squares) semisweet chocolate, coarsely chopped (optional)

Preheat the oven to 400°F. Line a baking sheet with parchment paper. Set aside.

Melt the butter in a small saucepan over medium-low heat. Add the brown sugar and cinnamon and blend well. Remove from the heat.

Place the tortilla on the prepared baking sheet and brush with the cinnamon mixture. (This step can be done up to 4 hours ahead. Cover with foil and allow to stand at room temperature.) Using kitchen scissors, cut the tortilla into 8 triangles. Bake

RECIPE CONTINUES

for 8 minutes, or until crisp. Remove the baking sheet from the oven and place it on a cooling rack.

Melt the chocolate, if using, in a small saucepan, covered, over low heat, stirring occasionally. (The chocolate can also be placed in a small dish, covered with plastic wrap, and set on the hot plate of a coffeemaker. Turn the coffeemaker on and the chocolate will melt slowly. Stir occasionally.) Once the chocolate has melted, remove the saucepan from the heat and tilt it at about a 45-degree angle to facilitate the dipping process. Dip the *wide* ends of the tortilla triangles, ½ inch up, into the melted chocolate and place each one on a piece of wax paper or parchment paper to set. Store the triangles in an airtight container at room temperature or in the refrigerator for up to 4 days or in the freezer for several weeks.

Cinnamon Wonton Crisps

These crispy, intensely flavored wontons are certain to become one of your favorite ways to garnish a smoothie—or any other creation you can conjure up just to have an excuse to make them. Making a slit in the wonton before frying allows it to be placed on the rim of the glass, or it can be inserted upright in the smoothie.

4 CRISPS

⅓ cup sugar
2 teaspoons ground cinnamon
1 cup corn oil
4 wonton skins

Line a baking sheet with a double layer of paper towels. Set aside.

Combine the sugar and cinnamon in a small bowl and blend well.

Heat the corn oil in a small, heavy saucepan over medium-high heat until the oil registers 350°F on a food thermometer.

Starting at one corner of each wonton skin, cut a slit halfway through to the center. Fry 1 wonton skin at a time, turning it over with tongs after 6 to 7 seconds, or until golden brown. (The wonton crisps will continue to brown after they are removed from the oil.) Using tongs, transfer the wonton crisps to

RECIPE CONTINUES

the prepared baking sheet and immediately sprinkle both sides with the cinnamon mixture. (Any remaining mixture can be kept in a covered container and used as needed.) Allow the crisps to cool. When the Cinnamon Wonton Crisps are cool, store them in an airtight container at room temperature for up to 2 days.

Crisp Banana Wafers

These crispy wafers are simply made of puréed
bananas that have been baked in a slow oven
until the mixture becomes brown and crisp. The
cooled baked banana purée is then broken into
irregular pieces that can be used to adorn any
of the smoothies found in this book.

12 TO 16 WAFERS

2 medium bananas, peeled and cut into 1-inch pieces
1 to 2 tablespoons sugar

Preheat the oven to 200°F. Line a baking sheet with
a silicone baking mat. Set aside.

Place the bananas and sugar in the workbowl of
a food processor fitted with a metal blade (or in a
blender) and process for 45 seconds, or until the
bananas are puréed. Spoon the puréed bananas in
the center of the prepared baking sheet. Using an
angular metal spatula or a straight spatula, spread
the purée evenly into a rectangular shape about
1/16 inch thick. The layer should almost cover the
mat. Bake the banana purée for 2½ to 3 hours, or
until brown and completely dry. Remove the baking
sheet from the oven, place another sheet over
the baked banana purée, and invert it. Gently
remove the silicone baking mat and allow the

RECIPE CONTINUES

baked banana purée to cool for 30 minutes to an hour. When the baked banana purée is cool, break it into irregular triangular shapes. The Crisp Banana Wafers can be stored in an airtight container in a cool, dry place for up to 2 days.

Peanut Butter – Chocolate Drops

This candy is all about obsessions: crunchy peanut butter and chocolate. Beware! When these heavenly morsels are combined with other sumptuous ingredients, the result is a deliriously delicious candy that is utterly addictive.

96 DROPS

2 cups crunchy peanut butter
¾ cup (1½ sticks) unsalted butter, at room temperature
1 box (1 pound) confectioners' sugar
3 cups Rice Krispies
96 6- or 10-inch wooden skewers
1 ounce household paraffin wax
1 7-ounce milk chocolate candy bar, coarsely chopped
1 6-ounce package semisweet chocolate chips

Place the peanut butter and butter in the large mixing bowl of an electric mixer and beat until light and fluffy. Gradually add the sugar and blend well, then stir in the Rice Krispies. Pinch off 1 tablespoon of the peanut butter mixture, roll it between the palms

RECIPE CONTINUES

of your hands to form a ball, and place it on a baking sheet. Repeat this process with the remaining mixture. Insert a skewer halfway into each peanut butter ball. Cover the baking sheet with aluminum foil and refrigerate for about 2 hours.

When you are ready to prepare the Peanut Butter–Chocolate Drops, melt the paraffin in a medium saucepan over medium-high heat. Lower the heat to medium-low and add the chocolates; blend well. (Paraffin wax is often added to chocolates—don't worry, it is edible. The addition of paraffin to the Peanut Butter–Chocolate Drops gives them a nice, glossy finish and helps them remain solid at room temperature.) Once the chocolates have melted, remove the saucepan from the heat and tilt it at about a 45-degree angle to facilitate the dipping process. Holding onto the skewer, dip each peanut butter ball into the chocolate, allowing the excess to drip back into the saucepan while gently twisting the skewers. Place each drop upright in a glass or on a piece of wax paper and allow the chocolate to harden. Remove the skewers and store the Peanut Butter–Chocolate Drops in the refrigerator or freezer for up to a month or two. If the drops have been frozen, allow them to sit at room temperature for 10 minutes before serving, then insert a long skewer into each one. Place a Peanut Butter–Chocolate Drop upright in the smoothie.

NOTE: The recipe can be easily cut in half, if eight dozen individual drops seems too much.

Pear Chips

Like their apple and pineapple cousins, Pear Chips are crunchy, paper-thin slices of tantalizing flavor. They add a sophisticated elegance to smoothies as well as other desserts. The chips are best when the pears are thinly sliced with a mandoline or vegetable slicer; however, with a little patience, a sharp knife can be just as effective.

10 TO 12 CHIPS

2 cups cold water
1 cup sugar
1 firm Bosc or red pear, unpeeled and uncored

Bring the water and sugar to a boil in a large saucepan over medium-high heat, stirring frequently to dissolve the sugar. Reduce the heat to low.

Meanwhile, use a mandoline or vegetable slicer to slice the pears into lengthwise slices about 1/16 inch thick, or as thin as possible (remove and discard any seeds). Add the pear slices to the water and sugar mixture, one slice at a time. Cook for 10 minutes, or until the pear slices are transparent. Remove the saucepan from the heat and allow the pear slices to cool in the syrup.

Preheat the oven to 275°F. Line a baking sheet with parchment paper or a silicone baking mat.

RECIPE CONTINUES

Using tongs, remove the pear slices from the syrup and place them in a single layer on the prepared baking sheet. Pat the slices dry with a double layer of paper towels. Bake the pear slices for 30 to 40 minutes, or until they are dry. (To test for doneness, remove a pear slice from the baking sheet and allow it to cool. If it is not crisp, then bake the pear slices a little longer, checking every 15 minutes to see if they're done.) The Pear Chips can be stored in an airtight container in a cool, dry place for up to 2 days.

Pineapple Chips

This garnish can elevate pineapple smoothies and many made with other fruits to a new dimension. The chips are deliciously sweet and look sensational when inserted upright into a smoothie. This is also a perfect garnish for a dish of sorbet or ice cream.

12 TO 18 CHIPS

1 fresh pineapple, top, bottom, sides, and
    core removed
1 cup sugar
1 cup cold water

Preheat the oven to 225°F. Line a baking sheet with a silicone mat. Set aside.

Using a mandoline or vegetable slicer, thinly slice the pineapple into horizontal rings about ⅟₁₆ inch thick, or as thin as possible. With patience, the pineapple rings can be sliced with a knife. Place the pineapple rings in a shallow roasting pan and set aside.

Bring the sugar and water to a boil in a heavy small saucepan over moderate heat, stirring occasionally. Pour the hot mixture over the pineapple rings and cover the pan with aluminum foil.

Place the pan over 2 stove burners; cook over low heat for 15 minutes. Remove the pan from the

RECIPE CONTINUES

burners and allow the pineapple rings to cool to room temperature.

Once the pineapple rings are cool, place them on the prepared baking sheet and bake for 60 to 90 minutes, or until they turn golden brown. Allow the Pineapple Chips to cool before storing them in an airtight container in a cool, dry place for up to 2 days. The Pineapple Chips will become crisp as they cool.

NOTE: As soon as the Pineapple Chips are baked, they can be kept whole, formed into a rolled cigar shape, or cut into wedges.

NOTE: The Pineapple Chips can also be made by thinly slicing the pineapple into rings and placing them on a double thickness of paper towels. Pat the tops of each pineapple ring with paper towels, then transfer them to a baking sheet lined with a silicone mat. Sprinkle $\frac{1}{4}$ teaspoon sugar over each ring and bake in a preheated 350°F. oven for 60 to 90 minutes, or until golden brown.

Strawberry Fans

Strawberry Fans add a nice touch of color when placed on the rim of a glass and are a tasty treat as well.

2 FANS

2 whole firm strawberries, unhulled

Using a very sharp knife, make 5 to 6 very thin vertical cuts through each strawberry, starting ¼ inch down from the stem end and cutting through to the pointed end. Place the strawberries on a plate and carefully spread the slices apart to resemble opened fans. Slip a Strawberry Fan over the rim of a glass.

Turtle on a Skewer

The recipe for this delectable treat is a variation of one that comes from my good friend Judy. You can insert a skewer into each turtle so it can be placed upright in a smoothie, or it can be simply served on a dish as an accompaniment to one of the many irresistible smoothies found throughout this book. Keep in mind that these chunky bites of sinful pleasures can be doubled in quantity by simply placing only one dollop of caramel instead of two on the prepared baking sheet for each turtle and only four pecans in an X design.

4 TURTLES

32 pecan halves
16 Kraft light caramels, unwrapped
1 teaspoon light cream
4 6- or 10-inch wooden skewers
1 2.6-ounce milk chocolate bar, coarsely chopped

Line a baking sheet with nonstick aluminum foil. On the upper left side of the baking sheet, place 4 pecans, flat side up, in an X shape. Repeat this procedure on each of the other 3 sections of the baking sheet. Set aside.

Place the caramels and cream in the top of a double boiler over simmering water on medium-high heat. Cover and cook for 8 to 10 minutes, or until the caramels are soft. Use a wire whisk to blend the mixture until smooth. Lightly coat a teaspoon with a nonstick vegetable spray. Using the spoon, drop a dollop of caramel over the center of each set of pecans and spread it partially over the pecans with your fingertips or a lightly greased spatula. (Place the top of the double boiler over the simmering water while doing the next step to keep the caramel mixture warm.) Place the pointed end of a skewer halfway on top of each caramel, parallel to the baking sheet. (If any pecans were moved out of the X shape, simply realign them.) Top each turtle with another teaspoon of caramel and place 4 pecans, flat side down in an X shape on top of the caramel, pressing down slightly. Allow the turtles to stand at room temperature for at least 30 minutes.

Melt the chocolate in a covered microwave-safe dish in the microwave on high for 40 to 60 seconds. Blend the chocolate until smooth. Using approximately half the chocolate in the dish, top each turtle with a spoonful of chocolate, spreading it completely over the caramel. After about 2 hours or once the chocolate has set completely, reheat the remaining chocolate in the dish. Turn the turtles over, chocolate side down, and spoon the remaining chocolate on each turtle, spreading it to cover the caramel. Allow the chocolate to set completely. If the turtles are not going to be served immediately, each one can be wrapped tightly in plastic wrap once the chocolate has set. The turtles will stay fresh at room temperature for up to 5 days.

RECIPE CONTINUES

NOTE: The original recipe, given below, is a quick and easy way to prepare these turtles, but one that produces a crispier candy. The ingredients are almost the same, except for one—it uses a chocolate kiss instead of a melted milk chocolate bar.

Simply preheat the oven to 300°F. Line a baking sheet with a piece of parchment paper or nonstick aluminum foil (or lightly grease the baking sheet). On the upper left side of the baking sheet, place 1 caramel in the center. Repeat this procedure on each of the other 3 sections of the baking sheet. Bake for 6 minutes, or until the caramels soften. Remove the baking sheet from the oven and place the pointed end of a skewer halfway on top of each caramel, parallel to the baking sheet. Place 4 pecans, flat side down, in an X shape on top of each caramel and top each with a chocolate kiss. Return the baking sheet to the oven and bake for 1 minute, then remove the sheet from the oven and place it on a cooling rack. Using a knife, swirl the chocolate over the caramel. Allow the turtles to sit at room temperature for several hours to let the chocolate harden. If they will not be used immediately, the turtles can be wrapped in plastic and stored at room temperature for up to 4 days.

Index

INTERNATIONAL CONVERSION CHART

These are not exact equivalents; they have been slightly rounded to make measuring easier.

Liquid Measurements

AMERICAN	IMPERIAL	METRIC	AUSTRALIAN
2 tbs (1 oz.)	1 fl oz.	30 ml	1 tbs
¼ cup (2 oz.)	2 fl. oz.	60 ml	2 tbs
⅓ cup (3 oz.)	3 fl. oz.	80 ml	¼ cup
½ cup (4 oz.)	4 fl. oz.	125 ml	⅓ cup
⅔ cup (5 oz.)	5 fl. oz.	165 ml	½ cup
¾ cup (6 oz.)	6 fl. oz.	185 ml	⅔ cup
1 cup (8 oz.)	8 fl. oz.	250 ml	¾ cup

Spoon Measurements

AMERICAN	METRIC
¼ teaspoon	1 ml
½ teaspoon	2 ml
1 teaspoon	5 ml
1 tablespoon	15 ml

Weights

US/UK	METRIC	US/UK	METRIC
1 oz.	30 grams (g)	8 oz. (½ lb)	250 g
2 oz.	60 g	10 oz.	315 g
4 oz. (¼ lb)	125 g	12 oz.	375 g
5 oz. (⅓ lb)	155 g	14 oz.	440 g
6 oz.	185 g	16 oz. (1 lb)	500 g
7 oz.	220 g	2 lbs	1 kg

Oven Temperatures

FAHRENHEIT	CENTIGRADE	GAS
250	120	½
300	150	2
325	160	3
350	180	4
375	190	5
400	200	6
450	230	8

Also by Donna Pliner Rodnitzky

SLIM SMOOTHIES
0-7615-2059-7 • $12.95 paperback

Looking for novel and nutritious ways to
enrich your diet without adding too many
calories or unnecessary fat? Well here you
go! This tasty collection of more than 130
ultra-nutritious and energizing low-cal
smoothies is the perfect complement to
your daily meal plan.

SUMMER SMOOTHIES
0-7615-3732-5 • $12.95 paperback

From revitalizing fruit and dairy
drinks to sweet-tooth specialties and
cocktail-hour delights, more than
130 easy-to-make recipes for cool,
refreshing concoctions perfect for
the good ol' summertime.

TIPSY SMOOTHIES
0-7615-2650-1 • $12.95 paperback

Great ideas for transforming more than
150 popular mixed drinks into delicious
cocktail smoothies. Pineapple Margarita,
anyone? How about a Mango Daiquiri?
Or even a Banana Split Martini?
Cocktail hour was never so flavorful!

ULTIMATE SMOOTHIES
0-7615-2575-0 • $12.95 paperback

From nourishingly nutritional
to decadently delicious, here are
Donna Pliner Rodnitzky's greatest
smoothie creations, including
Honey, I Ate the Banana Smoothie;
Oh My Papaya; Peach Blanket
Bingo; and more than 120 others.

THREE RIVERS PRESS • NEW YORK